LAURA CHRISTIANSON

The
Adoption
Decision

HARVEST HOUSE PUBLISHERS

EUGENE, OREGON

Unless otherwise indicated, all Scripture quotations are taken from the HOLY BIBLE, NEW INTERNATIONAL VERSION®. NIV®. Copyright © 1973, 1978, 1984 by the International Bible Society. Used by permission of Zondervan. All rights reserved.

Verses marked MSG are taken from The Message. Copyright © by Eugene H. Peterson 1993, 1994, 1995, 1996, 2000, 2001, 2002. Used by permission of NavPress Publishing Group.

Scripture verses marked NRSV are from the New Revised Standard Version of the Bible, copyright © 1989 by the Division of Christian Education of the National Council of the Churches of Christ in the USA. Used by permission. All rights reserved.

Names and identifying details in some personal stories herein have been altered in order to preserve the privacy of the individuals involved.

Cover photos © Grove Pashley / Brand X Pictures / Jupiterimages; Andrea Gingerich / iStockphoto; Roger McClean / iStockphoto; Che McPherson / iStockphoto; Luis Alvarez / iStockphoto

Cover by Abris, Veneta, Oregon

THE ADOPTION DECISION
Copyright © 2007 by Laura Christianson
Published by Harvest House Publishers
Eugene, Oregon 97402
www.harvesthousepublishers.com

Library of Congress Cataloging-in-Publication Data
Christianson, Laura, 1960-
The adoption decision / Laura Christianson.
    p. cm.
Includes index.
ISBN-13: 978-0-7369-2000-1
ISBN-10: 0-7369-2000-5
1. Adoption—Religious aspects—Christianity. 2. Adoption—United States. I. Title.
HV875.26.C47 2007
362.7340973—dc22

                                                                    2007002488

All rights reserved. No part of this publication may be reproduced, stored in a retrieval system, or transmitted in any form or by any means—electronic, mechanical, digital, photocopy, recording, or any other—except for brief quotations in printed reviews, without the prior permission of the publisher.

Printed in the United States of America

07 08 09 10 11 12 13 14 15 / VP-SK / 12 11 10 9 8 7 6 5 4 3 2 1

In loving memory of

My mom,
Margaret Hutchison
June 13, 1934–April 22, 2003

and

My friend and fellow adoptive mom,
Shari Wilson
October 31, 1960–August 31, 2004

CONTENTS

"A kaleidoscope of vignettes, facts, sage wisdom, practical suggestions, and biblical counsel."

—SANDRA GLAHN, BESTSELLING COAUTHOR
OF *THE INFERTILITY COMPANION* AND
WHEN EMPTY ARMS BECOME A HEAVY BURDEN

"If you need a mentor and friend to walk you through the adoption process—someone who's been there, done that, and wants to pave the way for others—open this book and start reading now!"

—BARBARA CURTIS, AUTHOR OF
THE MOMMY MANUAL AND *MOMMY, TEACH ME!* AND MOTHER OF
12, INCLUDING 3 ADOPTED SONS WITH SPECIAL NEEDS

"Does a great job investigating both the important and the not-so-obvious questions that can arise when you listen to God's call to adopt."

—DAN WILSON, RETIRED SEATTLE MARINERS
CATCHER AND ADOPTIVE DAD

"An absolute must-read...a practical and comprehensive guide that will make any adoption experience better for everyone involved."

—JOHN NARDINI, EXECUTIVE VICE PRESIDENT, DENALI FLAVORS,
MAKERS OF MOOSE TRACKS ICE CREAM,
AND ADOPTIVE FATHER

"Adoption is the purest form of Christ's mandate to love."

—KAREN KINGSBURY, AMERICA'S #1 INSPIRATIONAL AUTHOR
AND ADOPTIVE MOM

"A must-have book for anyone considering adoption. It is filled with extremely useful insights into this emotionally charged and uncharted territory. Reading it will definitely smooth out many of the possible bumps on the journey."

—RUTH GRAHAM AND SARA DORMON, PhD
COAUTHORS OF *SO YOU WANT TO ADOPT...NOW WHAT?* AND
I'M PREGNANT...NOW WHAT?

Home Improvement

Usually I awake to the cheerful chirp of robins outside my window. But one spring morning, the rumble of heavy equipment startled me out of slumber. I peered out the window and observed a herd of bulldozers on the property next to my home.

The inevitable had begun. The ten-acre horse pasture that bordered my quiet, rural cul-de-sac was being transformed into a 34-home development. That morning I took a long walk, digesting the fact that my life had suddenly morphed from "country girl" to "city girl." Living within inches of the newly created city limits would take some time to get used to.

It's that way with adoption too. When you decide to build your family through adoption, your "parenthood landscape" changes, and you begin to construct an entirely new mind-set. You excavate long-held beliefs in the importance of bloodlines and pour a new foundation, whose cement is love and commitment for a child with whom you have no genetic connection.

As you erect the framework for your nontraditional family, your anxieties and insecurities about adoption are exposed. You wonder whether you'll be able to love an adopted child as much as you'd love a birth child…whether adopted children come with money-back guarantees…how you'll integrate an adopted child into your extended family, your neighborhood, your world.

You face spiritual upheaval as well. You ask yourself if God has created the perfect child for your family—a child who is already out there, waiting for you. You wonder whether adopting means others will expect you to be a perfect parent. You mull over how adoption will test your faith.

Building a family through adoption is guaranteed to test and stretch you to the core of your being. The adoption process itself seems intimidating, but it becomes less so when you compare it with something familiar, such as home building. In fact, the adoption process mirrors the home-building process: You gather cost estimates, plan a budget, and obtain financing. You sign a contract and coordinate all aspects of the process with qualified professionals whose goal is to help you achieve your dream. You carefully design your home, prepared to make minor—or extensive—modifications to the plan. You wait—usually longer than you anticipate—for your home to be built. After your home is complete, you undergo a final inspection before you're approved to move in.

Just as it's impossible to visualize exactly what your home will look like before its completion, adoption also presents unique challenges that require you to modify and update your blueprint on a regular basis. While adoption manuals provide helpful information for navigating the adoption process, their one-size-fits-all instructions don't accommodate the creative touches you'll add to your family-building plan.

That's where this book comes in. *The Adoption Decision* is a "how-to for the heart"—a guide through the critical heart issues you'll encounter during the adoption process and after you bring home your child. As an educator, a journalist who loves to collect and share people's adoption stories, a Christian who has a lifelong friendship with God and His Word and—most importantly—a parent who lives the realities of adoption every day, I can offer you my insight and experience.

■ ■ ■

If you've ever designed a house, you've probably examined the house plans, furnishings, and decor of other homes, picking and choosing features that make your home uniquely yours. As you read this book, you'll have the opportunity to scrutinize "house plans" from dozens of adoptive families—newbies and veterans alike—as they share wisdom and advice gleaned from their experiences. While their names have sometimes been changed to protect their children's privacy, every story is true.

Their stories may startle you. These families, like any home under construction, are works in progress, fastened together with determination and strengthened with love. As you contemplate the blueprints of their lives, you'll begin to envision your own adoption floor plan.

You'll also delve into some historical records. People from the Bible experienced situations strikingly similar to the ones adoptive families encounter today. Whether you know very little about the Bible or it's an old friend, my hope is that the stories about men and women of the faith will sustain you during difficult days.

I encourage you to use the questions at the end of the book for individual reflection or group discussion. Consider passing this book along to extended family, friends, and colleagues as well. Your supporters are curious and apprehensive about adoption. They'll ask questions—lots and lots of questions. And because you're learning about adoption yourself, you may feel hesitant to explain something you don't yet fully understand. Throughout the book, you'll learn tips for acquainting your rooting section with adoption and teaching them how they can cheer you on during this critical juncture of your life.

It's time to gear up, home builders, and begin preparing for the best housewarming party ever. One day soon, you'll open the front door and welcome your new child across the threshold and into your family. And then you, too, will discover just what's so great about adoption.

Adoption Lingo

Adoption terminology can be confusing, especially in a book that contains references to both adoptive families and birth families. The following glossary will acquaint you with the terminology used throughout *The Adoption Decision*.

Adoption professional: an adoption social worker or case worker (I use the terms interchangeably), an adoption attorney, or an adoption facilitator. I use female pronouns to reference adoption professionals because the majority of them are female.

Birth parents: those who give birth to and release a child for adoption.

Child: adopted child. I use the qualifier "adopted child" or "birth child" only when distinguishing between the two for clarity's sake. When discussing children, I alternate between male and female pronouns.

Home study: A written assessment about a prospective adoptive family, compiled by a licensed adoption social worker. All prospective adoptive parents in the United States are required to participate in a home study.

Parent(s): adoptive parent(s).

Place or release a child for adoption: the process birth parents go through to relinquish their child.

Prospective parent(s): parent(s) seeking to adopt.

Referral: the information parents who adopt internationally receive about a particular child available for adoption. Referrals usually include photos and/or a video of the child, medical information, and any other known background information.

Travel group: Adoption agencies often arrange group travel for several of their families who adopt simultaneously from a particular region of a country.

We Need a Hero

It's a Bird! It's a Plane! It's...Supermom!

"Guess what? We're adopting!"

When my husband and I announced our intention to adopt, we heard one of two responses:

"You're a saint!"

"You're crazy!"

I mulled over the idea of achieving sainthood at age 32. It had a superhero-ish appeal. "Faster than a speeding bullet...more powerful than a locomotive...able to leap adoption agencies in a single bound. It's a bird! It's a plane! It's SuperSaintlyMom!"

Robert and I would rescue a homeless waif and our awestruck friends would treat us with new respect. We'd nod graciously in acknowledgment of their homage and smile Mona Lisa smiles as we calmly exhibited parenting skills far beyond those of mere mortals.

However, the fact that sainthood appealed strongly to my vanity excluded me from membership. So I pondered the second response to our adoption announcement: "You're crazy!"

I wondered, *Aren't all people who want to add to their families a little crazy?* When you choose to parent, you sign up for 18 years—minimum—of insomnia, worrying, and Costco-sized cases of Band-Aids. Why would anyone in their right mind want to add more stress to their life?

But would-be parents tend to gloss over those points. Instead, we imagine inhaling the sweet smell of our baby's skin; cheering our preschooler as she attempts to score her first soccer goal; visiting Disneyland with a wide-eyed youngster; demonstrating the finer points of toasting marshmallows over a campfire; and crying silent tears of pride as our teenager accepts her graduation diploma.

Adoptive parents are no more—or less—crazy than anyone who decides to parent. We just take a different route to get there. We conceive a child in our minds and hearts. During the first trimester of our "pregnancy," we prove our parenting fitness to assorted officials. And then we wait. And wait. Like elephants, our gestation period averages about 22 months.

Actually, being a little crazy is part of the adventure. There must be a lot of us slightly crazy people out there, because four in every ten Americans consider adopting a child. One million families actively seek adoption at any given time. And nearly 150,000 adoptions are finalized in U.S. courts each year.[1]

■ ■ ■

Many parents tell me they adopted because they took to heart the biblical mandate to care for orphans, to defend the poor and fatherless, and to rescue the weak and needy.[2] I applaud these parents and admire their altruism. I, on the other hand, adopted for the most basic reason. I wanted to become a parent. Manufacturing a baby via natural or medically assisted means wasn't an option for Robert and me, so we decided to create our family through adoption. Adoption was our second choice. It was a choice we sensed God leading us to and through. It was the best choice we ever made.

The Times, They Are A-Changin'

During the months Robert and I researched adoption, our perceptions underwent a slow yet radical shift. We had always thought

Ulterior Motives

■ ■ ■

Desiring to parent is a good starting point from which to begin exploring adoption. As you consider your motives for adopting, ask yourself whether you want to adopt because...

- your marriage is in trouble and you hope a child will bring you and your spouse together.

- you feel compassion for an orphan and assume that love alone is enough to meet a child's needs.

- you've made parenting mistakes with your other children and yearn for a second chance.

- you are infertile or your child died—and you believe that adopting a child, or replacing your lost child through adoption, will help you get over the pain.

- you want someone to care for you when you're old.

- you're lonely and hope a child will comfort you.

If you answered "yes" to any of the above, you might want to seek professional counseling before pursuing adoption. Adoption, in and of itself, adds an extra layer of complexity to a family. The best gift you can give a child is a healthy family and a healthy awareness of the unique challenges that accompany adoption.

adoption was great—for other people. Most Americans would agree: 63 percent say they have "very favorable" opinions about adoption. Overall, 94 percent say they approve of adoption.[3] But while public opinion of adoption runs high, there's widespread ambivalence that adopting is not quite as good as having a birth child: Only 50 percent of Americans believe it is very likely parents could love an adopted child as much as a child born to them.

"Will we be able to love an adopted child as much as we would love our birth child?" Robert and I asked each other. We weren't sure, since we had neither adopted nor birth children, but we were willing to leap into the unknown and commit to showering our adopted child with all the love we could muster.

Robert and I also agreed to resolve our fertility issues before pursuing adoption. "How strong is our desire to recreate ourselves?" we asked each other. "Is reproducing our primary goal? Or is creating a family our primary goal?"

That led to a discussion of nontraditional families. By adopting, we knew we'd open ourselves to being tagged as slightly odd or unusual. Even though the term *adoption* describes the legal procedure through which a child joins a family, the word is often used to label a person's character or personality: "He is *adopted*…Robert and Laura are *adoptive* parents." We suspected others would view us first as *adoptive* parents and second as parents, while we would view ourselves first as *parents* and then as adoptive parents.

Sixty-four percent of today's families do not fit the traditional *mother + father + 2.01 biological children = family* mold. Still, adoptive families are viewed by many as anomalies. Robert and I did some serious thinking about what constitutes *family*. We pondered today's society, full of divorced parents, single parents, stepparents, teen parents, interracial parents, foster parents, and grandparents who parent. We concluded that adoptive families seem quite ordinary when thrown into the smorgasbord of nontraditional parenting arrangements.

Spouse on Board

Robert and I committed to adopt almost simultaneously and in full agreement. But in many households, it's the wife who initiates the idea of adoption, the wife who researches it, and the wife encourages her husband to consider it. Several factors can divide spouses who are debating whether to adopt.

Ripe Old Age

"Is that your grandchild?" Adoptive parents, who frequently enter parenthood at a later age, are sometimes mistaken for grandparents. You may have taken a circuitous route to parenthood, opting first to climb the corporate ladder and become a homeowner. You may have experienced fertility challenges, and by the time you begin to explore adoption you're in your 40s or 50s. You may have recently married or remarried and desire to parent a child with your new spouse. Or you may have raised birth children and are now preparing for Round Two.

Whatever the reason, if you or your partner are in your late 30s or older, one of you is likely to resist adoption. You may have heard your spouse grumble, "I'm too old. I don't have enough energy to raise a child. By the time my child graduates from high school, I'll be retired, debilitated, or dead!"

If you're planning midlife parenthood, you must weigh additional factors when determining whether to adopt. While baby boomers are generally healthier and longer-lived than the preceding generations, midlife presents unavoidable physical challenges, namely a sluggish metabolism and hormonal changes that result in flagging energy. As a member of the "sandwich generation," you must anticipate caring for your aging or infirm parents while simultaneously raising children and preparing for retirement.

You must face the possibility that your child might not have grandparents for much of her life and that you might not live to see your child grow to adulthood. Your child's siblings and cousins—if there are any—will likely be much older. Older siblings make great babysitters, yet they may resent the new arrival, jealous that their place in the family seems threatened.

On the flip side, midlife moms and dads have the advantage of drawing from years of life experience. You're wiser and more comfortable in your own skin than your younger parenting counterparts. If you have previous parenting experience, you feel more confident in your abilities the second time around. And you generally have more time, tolerance, and financial stability to offer your child.

I know a couple who adopted their first child when they were in their early 50s. They now have four children. When I asked them how they felt about adopting at such an "advanced" age, they smiled and replied, "You're as old as you feel…and we feel young!"

Forfeiting Freedom

Hand in hand with the "I'm too old" complaint is the fear of losing your freedom. If you're firmly entrenched in your career you may balk at the idea of manipulating a packed work schedule or cutting back on business trips. If you revel in relaxing with a good book before enjoying a full night's sleep, the promise of endless sleepless nights may give you nightmares. If you volunteer frequently, travel on mission trips to far-flung locales, or take luxury vacations at child-free resorts, you'll need to brainstorm kid-friendly alternatives.

During the ten years before Robert and I became parents, we spent our summers traveling the world. We toured Australia and Scandinavia with our church choir, chaperoned high-school students on study tours to England and France, snorkeled in Hawaii, and attended world-class theatrical performances. Since our sons joined our family, our most exotic vacations have been such things as camping trips to Canada and a short-term mission trip to Haiti. When you add a child to your family you must decide whether you're willing to exchange your own meaningful, valued activities for new—yet still treasurable—memory-making activities you can enjoy together with your child.

Cash Crunch

A middle-income family with a child born in 2005 can expect to spend over $250,000 (adjusted for inflation) for food, shelter, and other necessities to raise that child over the next 17 years.[4] That figure doesn't include the cost of adopting the child, which can be substantial.

Unless you're quite wealthy, you'll need to adjust your lifestyle in preparation for adoption. Often, when a couple adopts, one spouse opts to trim a work schedule or quit a job in favor of staying home with the child. While the benefits of full-time parenting are innumerable, job realignment can be a budget-buster.

The year before we adopted our son Ben, I reduced my full-time teaching position to part-time. After we adopted Ben I continued teaching part-time for another year in order to save for adoption number two. Then I quit my teaching job and began a career as a freelance writer, taking on jobs that offered flexible hours and allowed me to work from home. During those first years of significantly-reduced income, we learned to invest wisely and live frugally.

You and your spouse will work through myriad issues en route to adoption. There are effective ways to encourage a reluctant spouse to jump on board with you. In *Adoptive Families* magazine, Jill Smolowe suggests a few:[5]

- Discuss your concerns, fears, and differences, listening to one another with interest rather than judgment.

- Understand that your spouse's initial reaction may not be his or her final reaction. Because adoption is an emotionally charged subject, your spouse needs time to thoroughly consider the issues.

- If you have trouble resolving your issues, seek counseling.

Praying with and for your spouse is critical. "Pray in the Spirit on all occasions with all kinds of prayers and requests," instructs the apostle Paul in Ephesians 6:18. When you're not sure what to pray for, the Holy Spirit will pray on your behalf, strengthen you with "a glorious inner strength," and fill you with His extravagant love.[6] As you and your spouse pray together, ask God to...

- direct your decision-making process

- help you agree about whether to proceed with adoption

- send encouragers who will support you as you proceed through adoption

- soften the hearts of loved ones who are opposed to adoption

- provide wisdom for the adoption professionals who advocate on your behalf

- comfort and direct your future child's birth parents

- protect your future child

Julie Wilson, an adoption counselor at Christian World Adoption in Charleston, South Carolina, says it's normal for one spouse (usually the wife) to jump on the adoption bandwagon first. She recommends that couples attend an adoption seminar to overview the process. At Christian World Adoption, for instance, the monthly seminars end with a visit by an adoptive family. "That is all it takes for some men," says Julie. "They talk with another man who has adopted. They see the ease within the family and they see that adopted kids are lovable kids like any child they would birth themselves." The connection with a living, breathing adoptive family eases many a reluctant spouse toward adoption.

Relative Confusion

The most prevalent concern prospective parents express is the possibility that relatives will resent them for adopting. One mom calls it "The Blank Stare." When Shari and her husband, Don, proudly announced their decision to adopt, they were greeted with The Blank Stare. "It was as if our family and friends couldn't quite comprehend what we could possibly mean by *adoption*," she says.

Every time Shari received The Blank Stare, she felt like bursting into tears. "If we would have told people we were pregnant, we would have gotten hugs, kisses and the normal round of good wishes." But adopting? That was another story.

Shari's sister offered a possible explanation for The Blank Stare, saying, "It's not every day you hear of people who are making plans to adopt."

Like Shari and Don, you may feel uneasy about the reaction you anticipate when you announce your intention to adopt. Some relatives have deep-seated biases against adoption based on negative experiences they've had or heard about. Others have ingrained race or class prejudices; one grandfather threatened to disown his adult daughter if she adopted from Guatemala.

Relatives and friends worry on your behalf, anxious that your child's background will present insurmountable challenges. Some are critical of adoption simply because their habit is to dole out criticism wherever they go. (One woman, upon learning she was going to become an adoptive grandma, shrugged and commented, "Well, if I have learned to love a dog, I can love anything.")

Most relatives and friends are uninformed about current adoption practices and feel insecure about their ability to process new information. One grandma who was invited to her daughter-in-law's baby shower announced that if her son and his wife could afford to adopt a baby, they could buy their own shower gifts.

As you ready yourself emotionally for parenthood, you'll probably wonder things like the following:

- *Will my child be accepted into the extended family?*

- *Will my child's grandparents shun him because he's a different race or because he doesn't share the family bloodline?*

- *Will they slight him by giving him less love and attention than their other grandchildren?*

- *Will Grandma cry every time she sees my child because she feels sad for his birth mother?*

Despite your questions, doubts, and concerns, you'll embrace adoption. But your relatives, who may be caught off guard by your Big Announcement, need additional processing time.

Break It to 'Em Gently

So, how do you make The Big Announcement? You could put off informing relatives until the moment you bring home your child, in hopes that Grandma and Grandpa will take one look at the new grandchild and go dotty over him or her. While this method can work, it can also backfire.

If you feel uncomfortable announcing your intention to adopt in person or over the phone, consider some alternative methods.

Write it. You can write an announcement letter.[7] It's not a cop-out. A letter gives your loved ones time to absorb your emotionally loaded news without the pressure of responding instantly. It also serves as an effective preventative measure for Open-Mouth-Insert-Foot disease.

Write your letter in an upbeat tone that conveys your personality and your excitement about adoption. Explain the process that led you to choose adoption. Anticipate the questions people will ask, and include a list of Frequently Asked Questions about adoption. If you have a sense of humor, use it; a light touch makes unexpected news easier to digest.

Print your letter on fancy stationery—life-changing news demands an elegant touch. Mail your letter first to VIPs (relatives and best buddies) and then to your larger circle of friends, neighbors, faith community, co-workers, long-lost college roommates, and your second cousin's best friend's brother.

Blog it. Journal your feelings and experiences on a Web log (better known as a *blog*). Blogging is an inexpensive, interactive means of sharing the latest news, posting pictures, addressing hot-button issues, and educating your supporters about adoption.

Most blog hosting services allow you to create passwords so only family members and close friends can access your blog. Or you can blog your story to the world in hopes of inspiring, encouraging, and educating other adoptive families.

Gift it. A third method of making The Big Announcement is through giving a gift to your supporters. Sally and Bryan Miller, who adopted their daughter Emily from China, created home-made boxes using Chinese paper-folding technique. Inside each box they placed trinkets from Chinatown: chopsticks, paper fans, prayer bead bracelets, tea, fortune cookies, and aromatic Chinese soaps. They also included the Tapestry Books catalog (which contains adoption-related books), red roses, and cards that displayed the Mandarin translation of the recipient's name. And of course, the Millers included the announcement of their daughter's pending arrival. "Everyone in our extended family got really excited when we personally delivered the gifts," says Sally.

Shout it. If you're feeling particularly brave, you can organize a family gathering during which you'll make The Big Announcement. Plan a festive occasion, complete with balloons and banners. If you anticipate opposition, invite a confidante who completely supports your adoption plan.

A Malady of the Mouth

"There is nothing worse than aggressive stupidity," wrote German philosopher Johann Wolfgang von Goethe. Adoptive families can fall victim to those plagued with this malady.

The Learning Curve

■ ■ ■

Help your supporters learn about adoption *with* you:

- Introduce relatives and close friends to the unique aspects of adoptive parenthood by inviting them to attend a workshop with you at an adoption conference, a local adoption agency, or via the Internet.

- Join a support group or an Internet discussion group for adoptive parents. Spending time with others who share similar experiences will help you understand that your challenges are not unique or unusual.

- Read adoption blogs. Bloggers relate firsthand experiences that educate and inspire you and your supporters.

- Subscribe to magazines such as *Adoptive Families, Adoption TODAY,* and *Fostering Families TODAY.* Send pertinent articles to your supporters.

- Buy books about adoption and create a family lending library.

- Enlist the help of family and friends to create a scrapbook, quilt, or other memento to welcome your child.

- If someone asks you what you'd like for a shower gift, request babysitting. During the first few months after your child arrives, you'll be as exhausted as any new parent. A night out will help you regain your equilibrium and will give your supporters a chance to bond with your child.

Jackie attended her church's annual mother–daughter tea with her adopted daughters and was horrified when the keynote speaker launched the presentation with adoption jokes. The speaker mentioned how, as the third child in her family, she didn't have many baby pictures. "I must have been adopted," she quipped. The speaker then relayed how her brothers had scared her by telling her she'd have to go back to her *real* family: "You aren't really in our family because you're adopted," they teased maliciously. As the speaker concluded her anecdote, she laughed uproariously at her own wit.

When my husband's parents attended their forty-fifth high school reunion, the emcee awarded a prize to the alum with the most grandchildren. My proud father-in-law waved his hand in the air. "We have 13 grandchildren," he volunteered.

"They only count if they're biological grandchildren," retorted the emcee. "Stepchildren and adopted kids don't count."

Adoptive families are superheroes in the sense that they must develop nerves of steel. During the time you're expecting, people will ask the usual questions, such as, "Is it a boy or a girl?" or "What are you going to name her?" You'll also hear questions like…

- Can you choose whether you want a boy or a girl?

- How old is the child you plan to adopt?

- Is he healthy?

- Can you return him if he's not healthy?

- Where's he from?

- What ethnicity is he?

- How will you integrate your child into our culture?

- Will you take him to visit his native culture when he's older?

- What do you know about his birth parents?

- Will you stay in contact with the birth parents?

- What if the birth parents decide they want him back?
- Is there a money-back guarantee if the adoption fails?

The Never-Ending Battle for Truth, Justice, and the Adoption Way

It's tough to face public scrutiny—and even opposition—to your choice to adopt. The book of Esther in the Bible portrays two members of an adoptive family who personify the motto, "When the going gets tough, the tough get going." The narrative recounts how Esther, a young Jewish orphan, and her adoptive father, Mordecai (her older cousin), expose a diabolical plot to exterminate all the Jews in the Persian Empire.

When the Persian king Xerxes decides he needs a new queen to replace the one who had disrespected him, he discovers the gorgeous Esther. Instantly smitten, he crowns her queen. Following Mordecai's advice, Queen Esther does not disclose her family identity and ethnic heritage to the king.

Five years after Esther becomes queen, Xerxes' right-hand man, Haman, devises a scheme to rid the empire of all Jews. Mordecai gets wind of the plan, alerts Esther, and urges her to plead with King Xerxes on behalf of her people.

Aware that entering the presence of the king without an invitation will likely result in her death, Esther nonetheless agrees to approach Xerxes. She unveils her Jewish heritage and in a respectful yet determined manner, convinces King Xerxes to shield the Jews from the results of his decree.

Though Esther and Mordecai aren't ridiculed for their adoptive father–daughter status, they *are* scorned for belonging to God's adoptive family. But rather than reacting to Haman's venomous attack against the Jews with bitterness, Esther and Mordecai act with respect. Esther employs a simple three-step method to educate Haman and King Xerxes about God's chosen people:

1. She defines who belongs to God's adoptive family.

2. She explains why the Jews feel they're being unfairly persecuted.

3. She asks the king to reconsider his viewpoint.

King Xerxes, who realizes he's been duped into believing a myth based solely on a bitter man's prejudice, overrides his previous decree. The evil Haman, meanwhile, is left hanging—literally.

Thankfully, you won't have to risk your life as Esther did in her attempt to preserve an entire nation. But when people question your motives for adopting, you can follow Esther's example. 1) You can clarify that the children you adopt are part of your family, fully and irrevocably. 2) You can explain that all parents share the same primary goal: to provide a loving, secure home for a child. And 3) you can acknowledge that all God's children are part of a world-wide adoptive family.

Remember to remain calm and try not to react defensively. Instead, view insensitive comments as an opportunity to educate others. Trust that "the Lord will fight for you; you need only to be still."[8]

■ ■ ■

As you journey towards adoption, you'll experience the thrill of excitement mixed with fear of the unknown. You'll learn everything you can. At some point, you will take a leap of faith, unsure about what's in store, but committing to devote the remainder of your life to the child you hope to add to your family.

The mere act of adopting will accord you superhero status in the eyes of some. But don't allow others' assumptions to pressure you into feeling as if you must live up to the superparent role. You are not a superhero. Nor are you a saint or a lunatic. You are a parent.

Susan and Curt, parents of a ten-month-old they adopted from Russia, learned this the easy way. One day, when their son awoke from his nap, he snuggled into Susan before drifting back to sleep.

"I knew right then we were meant to be a family," recalls Susan. There was no superhero-like metamorphosis. Just a sense of knowing she was the most fortunate mom on earth; that no matter how their son had arrived in their family, they had been blessed with a privilege that defies imagination—the privilege of parenting.

2

Attached at the Heart

Will the Real Parent Please Stand Up?

"Your son looks so much like you and your husband—he looks as if he could be part of your family."

"He *is* part of our family," I reply.

"You know what I mean," says my acquaintance.

I am silent. I do know what she means, but I figure I'll give the woman a chance to redeem herself. No such luck.

The woman continues blithely, "His curly blond hair...his blue eyes...the shape of his face...he resembles you so closely. You'd never know he's not your *real* child."

I take a deep breath. *Count to 10, Laura,* I silently remind myself. I conjure up my best polite smile and respond, "Josh *is* my real child. He's been a member of our family since the day we met his birth parents when they were seven months pregnant. Josh came to live with us when he was two days old. That's about as real as you can get."

People rarely comment about resemblances between us and our other son, Ben, who doesn't look a bit like Robert or me. I figure people avoid saying anything for fear of saying the wrong thing, or because they imagine Ben is the product of a divorce and remarriage.

Others, however, blurt out whatever pops into their heads. One day, a door-to-door evangelist stopped by. Ben (then two) squeezed between my legs and the door jamb and peeked at the stranger.

31

"He has Japanese blood in him, doesn't he?" asked the woman.

Taken aback by this pamphlet-free approach to evangelism, I stammered, "Yes." Ben is only one-eighth Japanese—just enough to grace him with an olive complexion, dark hair and eyes. This woman was sharp.

She examined me closely. "Are you part Japanese?"

"No."

"Oh, then your husband must have Japanese blood."

"No."

The woman perceived I wasn't going to cooperate so she whipped out her Bible and began pointing out passages about the kingdom of heaven. She probably thought I was a heathen.

Sometimes, when people comment on my children's looks, the fruit of the Spirit, like an overripe banana, blackens and turns mushy. One weekend, we attended church with friends we were visiting. After the service we introduced ourselves to the official friendly greeter. Upon spotting Ben (our "Japanese" son), friendly greeter person announced, "Your son doesn't look anything like either of you. Who does he look like?"

"The milkman," I deadpanned.

Assumptions, Assumptions

It's easy to overanalyze every innocuous question others ask about your family and wonder…

- Are people surprised when adopted children resemble their parents?

- Do they think we're trying to fool the world into believing our children are homegrown?

- Do they assume we can't have children of "our own"?

- Do they pity us, imagining we settled for second best?

- Do they believe we'll feel validated as parents if they can convince us our kids look like us?

After much dissection and obsession I concluded most people don't realize we already feel comfortable with our family structure. In fact, while it's great that one of our sons shares Robert's Scandinavian features, we feel honored that both our boys are miniature carbon copies of their birth parents. Our sons' expressive faces, their voices, and even their mannerisms are daily reminders of the precious gifts we have been given.

When I choose to keep our children's biological parentage confidential, people assume the boys are "ours." They remark, "Your sons don't look at all the same. Isn't it amazing how two kids from the same family don't look a bit alike?"

"Yeah—amazing," I agree.

Then there's a fellow soccer mom I met when Ben joined a new team. We moms were standing on the sidelines watching practice. "Ben's the tallest one on the team," she noted. "Did he inherit his height from your side of the family or from your husband's?"

"Neither. We adopted Ben—he inherited his height from his birth father."

"I shouldn't make assumptions," apologized the woman. "It's great that you know where he got his height."

That's all she said. *I need to be friends with this woman,* I decided. After practice, I pulled Ben aside and pointed to his teammate, who was walking toward the parking lot with his thoughtful, nonintrusive mom. "What's that boy's name?" I asked urgently.

Ben glanced at me quizzically. "That's Nick."

When we arrived home, I whipped out the player roster and found Nick's mom. We will become friends. I just know it.

Looks Ain't Everything

By now you're probably trying desperately to recall whether you've inadvertently uttered an offensive statement about adoption anywhere, anytime, to anyone. You probably have. I certainly have. I'll let you in on a secret: When Robert and I contemplated adopting, we wondered whether we'd be able to fully love a child who didn't emerge from our gene pool. But once we decided to adopt, we got prickly when others insinuated that genetic ties are the be-all and end-all marks of authentic familyhood. That's because, for adoptive families, physical resemblance ranks dead last on the priority list for determining family connectedness.

Homegrown kids don't come with guarantees they'll look or act like their parents, either. And sharing the same genes does not guarantee a loving family. Still, our society obsesses over genetic ties. We endlessly compare a baby's features with those of other family members: "She has her daddy's curly hair, her mommy's hazel eyes, Grandma's cheekbones, and Grandpa's long fingers." Parents and child "bond," and the baby who looks so much like Mom or Dad is enthusiastically welcomed into the family.

A similar phenomenon occurs with infants adopted domestically. Birth parents, who often select the family who will adopt their child, tend to choose families with whom they share an affinity—in looks, temperament, or educational background. It's not uncommon for these children to strongly resemble their adoptive parents. When families discover those resemblances it eases the child's transition into the family.

But what about children who don't resemble their parents? What about children whose ethnicity is different than their parents'? Are they destined to remain outcasts simply because they don't mirror Mom's nose or Dad's toes?

I don't think so. I've been married to the same man for 25 years and I can attest that biologically unrelated people possess the capacity to bond. Within the biblical marriage covenant, husband and wife become "one flesh."[1] They no longer function as two autonomous beings, but as one, joined together in love and commitment. Parents, likewise, choose to bond with their children and love them unconditionally, no matter whom the children resemble.

Henri Nouwen, a Catholic priest and prolific author, writes that our children are the most important houseguests we'll ever have. Whether we adopt them or birth them, our children are unique creations, separate from us.

One movie star took Nouwen's "houseguest" concept to heart. After experiencing the joy of parenting her adopted child, the actress decided to adopt again. But she didn't adopt a baby; she informally adopted grandparents for herself and her son.

The actress, whose biological grandparents are dead, met a grandmotherly woman at a fundraising event and was struck by her warm, loving demeanor. The actress visited the woman and her husband at their home and asked if she could adopt them as her grandparents. Incredulous yet honored, the couple agreed and have since been fully embraced into the woman's extended family.

The celebrity's adopting grandparents demonstrates her understanding of a key adoption concept: It doesn't matter who your child belongs to; what matters is who belongs to your child. The actress filled a hole in her son's life by finding people to belong to him.

Choosing to belong to your child—to value him for who he is, rather than who he looks like—will positively impact him. Your love and acceptance is a security blanket he can grab ahold of during the moments he most craves validation.

Blood Is Thicker Than Water...Isn't It?

I grew up in a "traditional" home, consisting of mother + father + birth children. Today, that scenario is the norm for less than half of American families. Instead, many families are a hodgepodge of biological and non-biological members who represent multiple ethnicities. Although adoption is emerging as a mainstream method for creating a family, many people assert that biological family members are of intrinsically greater value than nonbiological ones. "Blood is thicker than water," they declare.

The premise behind the saying (which originated in twelfth-century Germany) is that blood leaves a stain when it evaporates, whereas water evaporates without a trace. Thus, some deem "blood" relatives more connected than people who are not related.

The Bible offers a different perspective on the "blood is thicker than water" concept. Within its pages, we discover that God chooses us to be His adopted children. God's son, Jesus, gives us a new birth (adopts us into His family) and "an inheritance that can never perish, spoil or fade." This inheritance—eternal life—is ours because Jesus shed His blood to free us from our sins.[2]

When our heavenly Father adopts us in the spiritual sense, He blankets us with a true sense of belonging—to Him and to each other. On the last full day of His life, Jesus vividly demonstrated His intent to unite all believers. As He shared the Passover meal with His disciples, Jesus passed them bread and wine, saying, "This [bread] is my body, given for you. Eat it in my memory…This cup is the new covenant written in my blood, blood poured out for you."[3]

Today, Christians remember Jesus' broken body and shed blood whenever we share in the Lord's Supper (Communion, or the Eucharist). As we do so, God reaffirms His covenant to unify all believers as His adopted children.

> When we drink the cup of blessing, aren't we taking into ourselves the blood, the very life, of Christ? And isn't it the same with the loaf of bread we break and eat? Don't we take into ourselves the body, the very life, of Christ? Because there is one loaf, our many-ness becomes one-ness—Christ doesn't become fragmented in us. Rather, we become unified in him.[4]

The inheritance God bestows on us isn't passed down through bloodlines, but through the blood Jesus shed to provide us permanent release from our sins. The stain on our hearts is the mark of God's love—the sign of His desire to adopt each of us.

The "Real Deal"

If God, who adopted us, considers us His "real" children, it seems fitting that we, too, should consider adopted children "the real deal."

Jeanie, a Caucasian mom of two biracial children, is frequently asked whether both her kids are her "real" children. She cheerfully responds, "No, one of them is fake."

Not long ago, I found a great definition of adopted children:

Natural child: Any child who is not artificial.

Real parent: Any parent who is not imaginary.

Your own child: Any child who is yours to love.

Adopted child: A natural child, with a real parent, who is loved.[5]

Accepting an adopted child as a "real" member of the family means acknowledging both sets of parents who play an integral role in the child's life. Your child's first parents—commonly called *birth parents*—conceived her and nurtured her, at least during the months she was in the womb. If the birth father was involved, he actively parented as he supported his partner and helped plan for his child's future. As your child's "second" parent, you now cherish her, just as you would a birth child. You change hundreds of dirty diapers, push her swing for hours at a time, sing her to sleep every night, and pray for her. You are not a substitute parent. You are not a babysitter. You, like your child's birth parents, are a *real* parent.

"If we start to act like we think a real parent would, we eventually become one," writes Jana Wolff in *Adoptive Families* magazine. She stresses the importance of claiming the titles *Mom* or *Dad*: "Our sons and daughters are counting on us to be nothing less than the real thing."[8]

Uniquely You

While Robert and I are *real* parents to our *real* children, we simultaneously celebrate their genetic heritage. We delight in our

Love at First Sight...or Not?

■ ■ ■

Soon after Dan and Annie Wilson adopted their first daughter from Bulgaria, Annie got pregnant. A friend asked Dan whether he'd feel the same about his adopted daughter, Sofia, now that Annie was pregnant with "the real thing." Dan admitted, "I'm worried that I can never love another child as much as I love our Sofia."

While some parents insist they love their child "at first sight," loving a child isn't always as simple as turning on a faucet and watching the love flow. Bonding occurs naturally, over time. You can jump-start the process by choosing to love.

To love in this intentional manner requires intellectual, spiritual, and social discipline. First, you must prepare your mind for action. Second, you must have a reverent attitude toward God. Third, you must demonstrate a sincere love for others.[6]

As you work to develop this, God will encourage you with His love. The apostle John writes, "How great is the love the Father has lavished on us, that we should be called children of God! And that is what we are!" John then challenges believers to show they belong to God by practicing loving others.[7]

Love is a choice, and it's not always an easy one. Practicing the discipline of loving may mean lavishing attention on a child who has never been loved. It may involve being rebuffed by the very child you're trying so hard to love. But as you allow the bonds of love to ripen, you'll discover that your child fits as perfectly in your family as if she had been born into it.

sons, both of whom are so different from either of us. Robert and I are introverts. We're content to hang around the house, read books, and check e-mail. When we attend parties, we seek out the room with the fewest people in it.

Our son Ben, though, is often described as "the superball in a room full of bouncing balls." He knows the names of every student at school, and he's happiest when immersed in innumerable activities. Since Ben was an infant, we've marveled at this cheerful, happy-go-lucky boy whose demeanor was apparently instilled in his birth mother's womb. As Ben approaches adulthood, his personality has bloomed, yet remains consistent at its core.

Josh, too, retains the innate characteristics he inherited from his birth parents. When he was a baby, he'd rest quietly in our arms and smile at us. Josh has a gift for melting people's hearts—he even treats his Beanie Baby mouse as tenderly as if it was a real, live pet. While he sometimes gets scolded at school for being "too social," Josh's teachers tell us it's hard for them to get tough with him because he's so sweet.

Birth children are often different from their parents too. But parents seem mildly surprised when a child they've conceived does not mirror them. We adoptive parents *expect* our children to exhibit unique temperaments, talents, and physical traits. We're surprised when our children resemble us.

Despite the fact that Josh's personality matches ours more closely than does Ben's, both our sons have taught us a great deal about appreciating differences. We've learned that no matter how much we wish our sons would think like us, act like us, or react like us, it isn't going to happen. They challenge us, invigorate us, exasperate us, and make us laugh. They're teaching us to view life through their eyes, not just from our hazy perspective. I believe God planned that when He created Ben and Josh and orchestrated their entrance into our family. I celebrate my sons with the words of Psalm 139, as paraphrased in *The Message:*

You shaped me first inside, then out; you formed me in my mother's womb. I thank you, High God—you're breathtaking! Body and soul, I am marvelously made! I worship in adoration—what a creation! You know me inside and out, you know every bone in my body; you know exactly how I was made, bit by bit, how I was sculpted from nothing into something. Like an open book, you watched me grow from conception to birth; all the stages of my life were spread out before you, the days of my life all prepared before I'd even lived one day.[9]

Children truly are "marvelously made." You can affirm an adopted child's uniqueness by remembering a few simple pointers:

- When you feel compelled to speculate about whether a child's traits are the result of genetics or environment, do it privately. Verbalizing "nature versus nurture" comparisons in the presence of an adopted child calls attention to the ways in which she's different and may lead her to believe she doesn't belong. Avoid making comparisons such as, "You sure look like your daddy," or "You don't look *anything* like your daddy." Whoever the child looks like, she will fit in if you decide she'll fit in.

- Many children suffer abandonment issues before their adoption. Never threaten, "If you misbehave, Mommy and Daddy are going to send you back." Such threats, even when made in jest, traumatize children.

- Rather than comparing adopted and birth children within an extended family, be attentive and responsive to each child as an individual.

Most importantly, delight in learning with and from the children in your life. Every child needs to repeatedly hear the words, "You are a special person and I love you. I'm so glad you are a part of our family!"

Pass the Bucks

The Price of Parenthood

"You don't realize how much money you can save until you have to save it," says Colette Steele. She and her husband, Michael, raised $60,000 to adopt four children from Russia. "Once we decided to adopt, we never worried about how much it would cost—we simply planned how to get the money," says Colette.

The Steeles and three other families from their neighborhood—who adopted a total of eight children from Russia among them—joined forces to raise funds for their adoptions. One of their most successful efforts was a rummage sale. Two weeks before the sale, they created a flyer that requested donations and included information about Russian adoption. They distributed the flyer to 500 homes within a five-mile radius. The sale netted nearly $4000. "We split the proceeds and used the money to pay for a plane ticket home for each of the kids," says Colette.

How Much Did Your Kid Cost?

Every adoptive parent is occasionally asked, "How much did your kid cost?" Whether the inquirers are simply snoopy or they need to know how much to budget for their own adoption, most people are aware adoption can be costly. According to the National Adoption

Attitudes Survey, 50 percent of Americans believe that paying for adoption is a major concern for adoptive parents. Even though the median income of adoptive families with children under 18 is $56,000 a year (compared to $48,000 for families who birth their children),[1] most adoptive parents aren't wealthy. And with adoptions costing as much as $50,000 and averaging somewhere between $15,000 to $30,000, prospective parents usually do some serious financial wrangling in order to adopt.

Because you'll likely shell out large amounts of cash before bringing home your child, people will assume you "bought" your child. However, if you adopt through legal channels you don't "buy" a child; the fees you pay finance an array of services provided by the team of professionals who facilitate your adoption.

Adoption fees generally fund the following services:

- review of initial application to adopt
- locating children available for adoption
- locating birth parents
- professional counseling for birth parents (domestic adoption)
- education and counseling for adoptive parents
- pre- and post-placement visits by an adoption social worker to the prospective parent's home
- interim care after the baby's birth, if needed (domestic adoption)
- interstate fees
- mediating ongoing correspondence between birth and adoptive families during the child's life (domestic adoption)
- dossier and immigration processing (intercountry adoption)

- operating costs for the adoption professional, including rent, utilities, telephone service, postage, advertising, office supplies, insurance, printing

Other typical expenses associated with an adoption include the following:

- fingerprinting
- physical exam for prospective adoptive parents
- medical or living expenses or both for birth parents
- prenatal and delivery care for birth parents
- child's medical bills after birth
- legal representation
- printing of adoption portfolio (domestic adoption)
- advertising, Web-site design, toll-free number, postage, fax (domestic independent adoption)
- travel, lodging, food, vehicle rental, interpreter services, guides (to another country or to the birth mother's state)
- required donation to an orphanage, relief program, or foreign agency (considered a tax-deductible contribution)
- citizenship and immigration services application (intercountry adoption)
- document preparation, translation, and processing (intercountry adoption)
- travel visas (intercountry adoption)
- interpreters and guides (intercountry adoption)
- naturalization (intercountry adoption)

Adoption fees vary considerably, depending on whether you use the services of a public adoption agency, a licensed private adoption agency, or an intermediary such as an adoption facilitator, an adoption attorney, or a physician. Licensed adoption agencies—whether they're public or private—operate under strict standards and provide a full range of services, including the following:

- home-study preparation
- matching prospective parents with either a child or a person wishing to place their child for adoption
- counseling for birth and adoptive families
- post-placement services

Adoption Options

Public-agency adoption is the least expensive form of adoption. That's because state-run agencies usually place only children with special needs, defined as…

- ethnic minorities
- sibling groups
- older children (usually age 3 and older)
- children with medical, developmental, or emotional challenges
- children who have had prenatal drug exposure
- children who have been abused, neglected, abandoned, or have mentally ill parents

You'll pay minimal fees (and sometimes, no fees at all other than reimbursable court costs to finalize the adoption) and you may qualify to receive postadoption services and subsidies if your child requires ongoing therapy or special medical attention. Some states cover placement of a child in a group home or residential treatment facility if the child's condition justifies removal from the adoptive

No-Fee Adoption

■ ■ ■

Antioch Adoptions in Redmond, Washington, touts *no-fee* adoptions. Antioch families pay no application fee, no home study fee, and no pre- or post-placement fee. The only fees they typically pay are attorney fees for adoption finalization (which are usually reimbursed) and for a weekend training retreat, says Executive Director Tammie Snyder.

Close to 60 percent of Antioch's families—while not required to do so—give back to the Christian ministry through donating their time, talents, and financial resources. They organize events, donate graphic design skills, act as speakers and co-trainers, and offer personal support to other Antioch families across Washington State.

Tammie notes Antioch has eight staff members and explains, "We pay our staff. We have lights and heat." But while there are costs to adoption, "there shouldn't be exorbitant costs that prevent families from stepping forward," she says.

As a result of its no-fee philosophy, Antioch sees many repeat families; some adopt three or four children. "When money isn't a barrier, families are more inclined to continue adopting," says Tammie.

home. If you adopt through a public agency, you must negotiate and sign adoption support agreements before the adoption is finalized.

Licensed private-agency adoption. Private agencies often contract with public agencies to place children who are waiting to be adopted. In addition, private agencies specialize in intercountry adoptions, domestic infant adoptions, and transracial adoptions. Adoption fees cover an array of services, and fees vary widely among agencies and even among programs within a particular agency.

For example, one mid-size agency charges $17,000 for adoptions from China, $25,000 for adoptions from Guatemala, and $20,000 for domestic healthy infant adoptions.

Another agency charges $6000 for adoptions from China, $19,000 for adoptions from Guatemala, and $18,000 for domestic healthy infant adoptions.

A third agency charges $9000 for adoptions from China, $22,000 for adoptions from Guatemala, and $20,000 for domestic healthy infant adoptions.

Many agencies have contingencies in place should an adoption fall through. They may refund some of the fees, and they continue working on your behalf—at no additional charge—until an adoption is completed.

In **private or independent adoption** (which is illegal in several states), prospective adoptive parents and birth parents find one another directly. Alternately, individuals such as physicians, attorneys, clergypersons, or professional adoption facilitators match those hoping to adopt with those planning to relinquish a child. Once the match is made, the intermediary usually connects both parties with an adoption attorney and with an adoption agency or social worker who completes the required home study.

Adoption facilitators tout lower fees and shorter waiting periods than adoption agencies, but they also represent greater financial risk for adoptive parents. For example, you may pay a prospective birth mother's living expenses and medical bills during her pregnancy and delivery. If she decides to parent her baby you usually do not receive your money back. In addition, facilitators do not operate under the rigorous licensing standards required of adoption agencies. Therefore it's critical that you select a competent, ethical facilitator and/or adoption attorney who has a stellar reputation within the adoption community.

Show Me the Money

Whether you use the services of an agency or a facilitator, you'll typically pay adoption fees over a period of months. First, you'll pay a non-refundable *application fee,* which usually ranges from $50 to $200.

Many adoption service providers charge an *education fee* that covers the pre-adoption orientation and training you'll receive.

Program fees are also common; they cover the expenses generated within a specific program (such as African–American adoption, infant adoption, or programs for particular countries, such as India, Haiti, or Russia).

Next comes the *home study fee,* commonly called the *family preparation* or *assessment fee.*

You'll pay the bulk of the fees when you receive a referral or are "matched" with a child. You'll make the final payment after your child is placed in your home.

Adoption service providers—many of whom are adoptive parents themselves—understand the challenges of financing adoption. Most offer some form of financial assistance, such as sliding-scale fees based on your family income. For example, an agency may base its fees for domestic infant adoption on a percentage of your family's total adjusted gross income averaged over the three most recent tax years.

Some adoption service providers offer interest-free adoption loans and subsidies for families who adopt children with medical or behavioral challenges, older children, members of a sibling group, or children of color. Other agencies partner with financial institutions to offer low-interest lines of credit.

As you debate which adoption professional to work with, compare the fees and services offered; adoption professionals often charge drastically different fees for the same services. Chart the range of prices each provider quotes. That way, you'll have a visual baseline from which to compare fees and services. If a fee seems out of the ordinary, ask about it when you interview the adoption service provider.

Be sure to obtain a written explanation of services the stated fees will and will not cover. Ask to negotiate a payment plan. Finally, be wary of adoption service providers who accept you without first reviewing your application or who require full payment up front without any provisions for a refund should they not find a child for you.

Finding the Finances

Though the expenses involved with adoption can be large, there are also many resources to help with the money needed.

Workplace Benefits

As adoption becomes commonplace, more employers are providing adoption benefits. Nationally, around 20 percent of companies (and about 40 percent of large companies) offer adoption assistance programs ranging from full or partially paid adoption leave to financial aid packages. On average, companies that provide adoption benefits allocate around $2000. They most often cover legal fees, birth mother medical costs, and agency and placement fees.[2]

The Adoption-Friendly Workplace, a resource center for advocates of workplace adoption benefits, recommends strategies you can use to convince your employer to offer adoption assistance.[3] Samantha Kitch successfully lobbied her employer to provide an infertility and adoption benefits package. "I researched what my company did and didn't cover," says Samantha. "Then I sent a petition around the inner office and asked women to sign it."

Samantha forwarded her petition to the corporate manager in

charge of benefits, highlighting the company's family values mission and explaining how infertility and adoption benefits would facilitate family building for people like her. A couple of years later, her employer began offering a benefits package that included a $4000 adoption reimbursement and $10,000 in lifetime infertility coverage. The benefits helped Samantha and her husband, Randy, to afford adopting a child and birthing two children through embryo adoption and donor eggs.

Other workplace benefits for adoptive families include the Federal Adoption Tax Credit, the Family and Medical Leave Act, and the DoD Adoption Reimbursement Policy (for members of the Armed Forces). As of 2007, the Federal Adoption Tax Credit reimburses eligible adoptive families up to $11,390 per child for specific adoption-related expenses.[4]

Under the Family and Medical Leave Act, employers of 50 or more people must grant eligible employees up to 12 workweeks of unpaid leave upon placement of a foster or adopted child.

Active-duty military personnel are also eligible for reimbursements of up to $2000 per child (up to a maximum of $5000 per calendar year), and they receive up to 21 days of adoption leave.

Subsidies, Grants, and Corporate Donations

Parents who adopt hard-to-place children with special needs may be able to take advantage of federally-funded and state-funded subsidies. Under the Federal Title IV-E Adoption Assistance Program, your financial status is not a factor in determining your child's eligibility to receive assistance. But not all children who receive state adoption assistance are eligible for federal funds.

Both federally-funded and state-funded subsidy agreements must be negotiated *before* the adoption is finalized. If you think you might be eligible to receive an adoption subsidy, ask your adoption service provider—early in the adoption process—to explain the details of the state and federal programs and to assist you with the necessary paperwork.

If you've pursued every option imaginable for funding your adoption and finances are still a barrier, consider applying for a grant. Grants are one of the least-known sources of financial assistance for people who adopt.

Some foundations that distribute grants are affiliated with particular adoption agencies and assist only clients of the agency. Shaohannah's Hope, for example, is dedicated to assisting Christian families; they give priority to parents who work with one of nine Christian nonprofit adoption agencies. Other foundations, such as the Gift of Adoption Fund, are not affiliated with a church or a social service agency and they work with all qualified applicants.

Organizations that distribute adoption grants prefer you approach them as a last resort—after your home study is complete and after you've exhausted other means of obtaining financial assistance. Perhaps you've sunk tens of thousands of dollars into infertility treatment and are scrambling for a few thousand to complete an adoption. Perhaps you intended to adopt one child and discovered siblings you'd also like to adopt but for whom you haven't budgeted. If you've already put tremendous effort into making the adoption happen and need a boost over the last financial hurdle, you just might become the fortunate recipient of a highly-coveted adoption grant.

Julianna Wiseman sidestepped the fierce competition for grants by soliciting corporate donations. Julianna, a single parent of 13 children from Guatemala and Russia, launched a letter-writing campaign, outlining her story and requesting donations of money or services from corporations and cultural groups. "I asked for whatever they would be willing to give," says Julianna. "Every company I approached donated cash or services such as medical insurance or dance lessons."

Julianna recommends the public library's reference section as a great place to research foundations, corporations, and nonprofit groups that might be willing to donate funds.

Benevolent Funds

Churches are another potential source for adoption assistance. Many churches set aside discretionary funds—often called deacons' funds or benevolent ministries—to assist people with short-term needs. These funds are separate from the church's general operating budget; those who wish to donate to them designate their contributions specifically to the fund. The funds are then distributed as needed among members and friends of the congregation.

Some churches establish adoption ministries (sometimes called "orphan ministries" or "waiting child ministries") that provide grants to families within the church. Dina and Heath Slack received a $1000 grant from their church's adoption ministry. "We prayed steadily through our most recent adoption concerning financial assistance and the Lord provided in an awesome way," says Dina.

Many church leaders and members are unaware of how costly adoption can be. But when they understand the expense involved, they often give generously to support those building families through adoption. "Any gift, no matter what amount, is a blessing," says Dina. "All the gifts we received played a part in helping us bring our daughter home from Taiwan."

Creative Fundraising

In addition to tapping into grants, loans, retirement accounts, and workplace benefits, you can creatively finance adoption. Angie Weldy, owner of AffordingAdoption.com, says that a well-organized fundraising event can net several thousand dollars in a short amount of time. One of her favorite fundraisers is "Pamper Day," in which a hair stylist, a cosmetics consultant, a massage therapist, and a caterer donate their services. Each Pamper Day attendee pays between $25 and $40 for a makeover, a massage, a manicure or pedicure, and a hair trim or style. The caterer provides snacks, and everyone enjoys a relaxing day.

"It's a win-win circle of goodness," says Angie. "It's good publicity for the people providing the service, a fun day to hang out with friends, and the adoptive mom raises money for the adoption."

When brainstorming fundraisers, ask yourself what type of fundraiser you'd attend and plan a fun fundraiser that provides value and brings a good return, advises Angie. Consider the following ideas:

- Host a fundraising dinner and auction for which friends sponsor a table and guests pay $10 per plate. Solicit goods and services from restaurants, theatres, and contractors for the auction.

- Ask friends and co-workers to donate gently-used books, DVDs, and CDs and sell them at an online auction. In the auction description, mention that proceeds will be routed to your adoption fund.

- Host a Bunko night and charge $10 a head. Rather than giving cash prizes to the winners, award inexpensive door prizes and add the proceeds to your adoption fund.

- Host a "Crop Till You Drop" scrapbooking party. Similar to the Bunko night, charge $10 to $20 for each attendee. Invite a scrapbooking consultant to demonstrate the latest techniques, help people with their pages, and sell her products in exchange for her donating a portion of the evening's sales to your adoption fund.

- Sell items you make at a craft fair, on consignment at a retail shop, or online. Since sales from handcrafted items trickle in over time, this fundraiser is most successful if you anticipate a long wait for your child or if you need a creative outlet to prevent you from going bonkers during the wait.

- Host a bike-a-thon, walk-a-thon, or skate-a-thon. Ask people to sponsor you or to solicit their own sponsors and join you for a ride, walk, or skate.

- Ask a bowling alley to donate several hours on a slow day. Invite friends to join you for an afternoon of bowling for a minimum donation of $10. Provide snacks and beverages and raffle wacky prizes.

- If you're adopting internationally, ask friends and family to pledge a dollar per mile to help you bring your child home.

Sacrificial Saving

If you despise fundraising and vow to stay out of debt when adopting, there are other alternatives. Members of the Internet-based group Frugal Adoptions live frugally in order to fund their adoptions.

Michele Eager, the mother of two birth children and a daughter adopted from China, didn't feel comfortable fundraising or soliciting donations from friends, family, and church members. She decided to start a forum for "tightwads"—those who share her theory that "small pennies add up." Michele believes that if you temporarily change your spending habits you can save at least half the money you'll need to adopt within one year.

As soon as you begin dreaming of a child, begin saving and living as if your child is already with you, Michele recommends. If you are a two-income family, live as if you are a one-income family, socking away a significant portion of one salary into a "child" fund. Work overtime whenever possible or moonlight for a few months. Designate a set amount each week to be deducted from your paycheck and directly deposited into your "child" account.

Grocery shopping is a "huge savings factor people overlook," says Michele. She advises would-be tightwads to take The Pantry Challenge. "Rather than running out to buy groceries, get creative with what you have in the pantry. Cook in rather than eating out. Or limit eating out to once a week, and patronize the local pizza parlor that offers half-price pizza on Tuesdays."

The members of Frugal Adoptions aren't anti-fundraising, notes

Michele. Many live frugally in order to supplement fundraising, or they haven't been successful with fundraising and seek an alternative. "Frugal living is an area that gets forgotten, but it, too, can play a role in helping someone to adopt."

Colette Steele's family developed "an attitude of sacrifice" as they schemed ways to adopt four children from Russia. "We cashed out our savings and sold our camping trailer," says Colette. Their five birth children volunteered to forego piano, gymnastics, and soccer until their siblings arrived; the kids collectively raised $1000 through babysitting, lawn mowing, and bake sales.

Raising the money to adopt four children simultaneously was faith-growing, says Colette. After she and Michael brought their children home, the family struggled financially for several months. But then a "cheap piece of land" they owned went commercial when developers decided to build a hospital next to it. "We sold it and paid off the adoptions," Colette says.

She and Michael didn't become aware of the potential to sell their land until after they had made the financial sacrifice to adopt their children. "It made me realize God was helping us along the way," she says. Colette and Michael received an additional blessing two months after they brought home their children; Colette got pregnant. The Steeles are now a happy family of 12.

Joyful Giving; Priceless Reward

The children we welcome into our family are God's greatest gifts—gifts for whom we willingly sacrifice our time, our energy, and our finances. King David exemplifies the virtue of joyful giving when he commissions his son, Solomon, to build a temple for the Lord. David wholeheartedly hands over all his personal resources to finance the construction of God's house.[5]

God delights when we give our financial resources—cheerfully and unreservedly—to continue building His house through adopting His children. The One who examines our heart and understands every motive behind our thoughts encourages us to hang in there, just as David encouraged Solomon:

> Be strong and courageous, and do the work. Do not be afraid or discouraged, for the LORD God, my God, is with you. He will not fail you or forsake you until all the work for the service of the temple of the LORD is finished.[6]

Throughout your child's life, you'll offer a thanksgiving sacrifice to God every time you marvel at the wondrous love He pours out; every moment you pass God's love on to the next generation of His family. All God asks of you is a willing heart that proclaims, "Oh God, here I am, your servant, your faithful servant: set me free for your service!"[7]

While financing your adoption will challenge you, don't allow cost to discourage you from adopting. Invest your heart in adoption, and God will help you find a means to bring home your priceless child.

4

Labor of Love

Pregnant Without
a Due Date

I plopped my Bible and notebook on the table and shrugged out of my jacket. The church classroom hummed with chatter about ultrasounds, labor pains, and breastfeeding. Glancing at the eight-months-pregnant woman on whom the conversation focused, I decided it was time to make my own announcement. I took a deep breath. "I'm expecting a baby, too." A dozen heads swiveled my way. "My husband and I are adopting."

"Oh, you're having your baby the *easy* way," remarked the pregnant woman, rolling her eyes at the group. I felt like melting into the floor.

Most people wonder how adopting can possibly equal the hardship of pregnancy and labor. After all, when people decide to adopt, their names are put on a waiting list. When their names reach the top of the list, they're presented with a gift-wrapped child. Right?

Wrong. That's like assuming that when people decide to have a baby, they make love once, get pregnant, and nine months later, out pops a baby. In the real world, expecting a child—through birth or adoption—is much more complex.

In *The Great House of God,* Max Lucado writes, "I've heard of unplanned pregnancies but I've never heard of unplanned adoptions." For those who build a family through adoption, the term "family planning" takes on a whole new meaning. Like all potential parents, we first ponder parenthood. We weigh the emotional, physical, and financial costs. Then we actively pursue parenthood.

At this point, the roads to biological and adoptive parenthood diverge. In *10-Minute Time-Outs for Moms,* Grace Fox introduces the "job description" of a pregnant mother-to-be:

> Must endure nausea for several weeks or months at the job's outset. Must tolerate her body stretching to unbelievable dimensions. Must withstand excruciating pain to deliver the fruit of her labor.[1]

Adoptive parents, on the other hand, experience a subdued "pregnancy"; most people don't even realize we're expecting. That's because the physical signs of pregnancy are missing: we aren't nauseous (although completing reams of paperwork can cause heartburn). We don't gain 40 pounds (just 10 pounds of worry weight). We aren't any crankier than usual (well, maybe a little). Our "pregnancy" might include overseas travel to meet our child, overnighters with a foster child, or overland trips to visit the prospective birth parents of our unborn child.

Our labor pains are psychological, rather than physical. Our children aren't delivered by doctors, nurses, or midwives, but by social workers, attorneys, and miscellaneous government officials. Despite the lack of a physical manifestation of pregnancy, expecting a child through adoption is every bit as important and life-changing as expecting a child through birth.

Supermom Returns

Just when I assumed I had come to terms with the whole Supermom syndrome ("You're adopting! Aren't you Super!"), it mutated like a comic-book villain and reappeared when my husband and I began what is officially known as the adoption home study. Or as most adoptive parents refer to it: The Dreaded Home Study.

The home study is a written report about your family compiled by an adoption social worker. Sounds innocuous, doesn't it?

But this is no mere report. This report evaluates your mind-set for motherhood, your philosophy on fatherhood, your proclivity for parenthood. In order to receive a passing grade on this report, you must convince a bunch of faceless bureaucrats you will be Superparent. Like most prospective adoptive parents, I felt a tad resentful about the parental certification exam. In *An Empty Lap,* Jill Smolowe articulates my annoyance:

> Some infertile couples want to know how it is "that any unmarried, drug-addicted, alcohol-swilling, shoplifting, truant teenage girl who gets knocked up by mistake" can raise that baby, no questions asked. Yet, when a mature adult whose only crime is an inability to reproduce wants to adopt a child, the operating assumption is that he or she is a child abuser, baby killer or vendor of infant body parts.[2]

My annoyance didn't lessen when, during our pre-home study screening, the adoption agency's social worker—who was supposed to lovingly guide Robert and me through the process—appeared to be conspiring against us. She repeatedly grilled us: "Are you *sure* you've come to terms with your infertility? Are you *absolutely certain* you want to create your family through adoption?"

I wanted to scream, "Yes, we're sure! Just let us get on with it, already!" Instead, I nodded and smiled through gritted teeth.

Then she asked us how we felt about the woman who'd give birth to our child. Since we hoped to adopt a newborn, we knew we'd have a close encounter of the most terrifying kind with pregnant people who would decide whether we would achieve our dream. It didn't feel fair, somehow, that unknown people would wield so much power over us.

With only a vague idea of what to expect about parenting, birth parents, and adoption in general, Robert and I focused on proving we were not child abusers, baby killers, or vendors of infant body parts. Determined to cling to a minuscule vestige of control, we poured ourselves into the home study.

Years later, as I reflect on the home study that loomed so large in our minds, I realize it was a mere blip on the screen of our lives—a means to an end. The effort we invested in our home study was worth it; we more clearly discerned our motives for adopting and we endlessly discussed potential parenting strategies. Although the fingerprinting, financial statements, and form-filling-out were not fun, our labor resulted in the addition of two delightful boys to our family.

So, exactly what hoops must you jump through to earn your "Certified Adoptive Parent" certificate? Let's wend our way through the world of The Dreaded Home Study and find out.

Skeletons in the Closet

What if they won't let me adopt? You may wonder whether disclosing ghosts from your past or youthful indiscretions will cause your application to get turned down. Don't let that stop you from applying. "There are very few insurmountable issues that prohibit a person from adopting," says Diane Lostrangio, a licensed clinical social worker and 16-year adoption professional. Adoption social workers aren't looking for ways to reject you. Their goal is to confidently recommend you for adoptive parenthood.

Whether you live with a chronic medical condition or physical challenge; have battled depression; abused drugs or alcohol; been arrested; don't own your home; are divorced or single; young or old; poor or wealthy; fat or thin, chances are good you'll be allowed to adopt.

"The intent of the home study is to screen out people with severe mental illness, drug or alcohol dependency, a criminal record of child abuse, or those with so little income that an adopted child would be placed into poverty," writes Mardie Caldwell in her book, *AdoptingOnline.com.* The home study may also eliminate those who have serious health problems that affect their life expectancy. She writes,

> If your home life is stable, if you are in reasonably good health, if you have enough income to raise a child, if you are a loving and responsible person with a heartfelt desire to parent a child for life, you can usually adopt.

Social workers are aware that everyone faces adversity, adds Diane Lostrangio. "Your social worker is most interested in learning what your particular life experiences are and how they might affect your parenting." If you withhold information and your social worker notices inconsistencies or suspects you're being untruthful, the negative impact will be compounded.

Sheri and Lyle Hatton, who are in the process of adopting a child from Ethiopia, worried about "getting past the social worker" who had the power to veto their adoption. Deciding honesty was the best policy, they shared openly. "Our social worker gave us the opportunity to fix areas of concern so those issues wouldn't hinder us from approval," says Sheri.

If your social worker feels uneasy about your readiness to adopt, she won't wait until the home study is complete and write a "bad" report; she'll share her concerns with you early in the process. She may ask you to resolve issues that could impact your parenting before you move ahead with adoption, and she'll help you locate professionals with whom you can work through those issues.

One of the signs of a good parent is the ability to deal with adversity. When you meet with your social worker, candidly describe the ways in which you've navigated difficulties. Your honesty will help your social worker feel confident that when parenting throws you curveballs, you'll whack them out of the ballpark.

Take Your Pick?

After you exorcise ghosts from your past, you'll need to establish boundaries around what "kind" of child you will and won't accept. "But I'd take *any* child," you protest.

Social workers know otherwise. "Adoptive parents back out of adoption at the last minute three-to-four times more often than birth mothers," says Mardie Caldwell. During her 20 years as an adoption professional, she's heard the following excuses from prospective adoptive parents:

- "I have a vacation planned when the baby's due."
- "The birth mother is a redhead and I don't want a red-headed child."
- "The birth mother is short and we're tall."
- "We'll only take a girl."
- "I don't like the birth mom's nose."
- "The baby's skin is too dark—he won't blend in with the rest of us in family photos."

Perhaps these scenarios could be eliminated if would-be parents took more care to express their preferences. While it may seem politically incorrect to set parameters, doing so is critical; the information you provide enables your social worker to find a child who will be a good fit for your family.

Before you check off the list, learn about the traumas institutionalized children and foster children typically face. Prayerfully consider whether you feel equipped to parent a child who…

- has physical, mental, emotional, or developmental challenges
- has a family history of mental illness
- has a family history of alcohol or drug abuse
- has a family history of genetically-related illnesses

- has a birth mother who received little or no prenatal care
- has a birth mother who is HIV-positive
- has a birth parent with a criminal record
- has no medical history records
- was born prematurely
- had prenatal exposure to drugs, alcohol, or other toxins
- has been abused or neglected
- has a different ethnic heritage
- has physical characteristics very different than yours
- is beyond babyhood
- lived in foster care
- lived in an orphanage
- has birth siblings who live with either the birth parent(s), with another adoptive family, or in foster care
- has no birth father identifiable or available to sign relinquishment documents (domestic adoptions)
- has birth parent(s) who want to remain in contact with their child
- has birth parents(s) who live either very close or very far away

The burden of checking off this list is heavy. In her memoir, *Two Little Girls,* Theresa Reid reflects that prospective parents are forced to express their desire for a child as a series of "No's":

> With every check mark we made in the "No" column, we felt criminally deficient in the capacity to love, in generosity of spirit. With each "No" we checked, the image of

a specific child floated before our eyes, a child we would refuse to consider even trying to love.[3]

If you eliminate too many possibilities, your chances of being matched with a child might decrease. If you don't eliminate any possibilities, you might end up adopting a child whose issues you aren't prepared to deal with. In *Carried Safely Home,* Kristin Swick Wong eloquently captures the dissonance parents feel as they examine the checklist:

> I hated to deliberately turn down a child with special needs, a precious child created by God who would doubtless bring us all great love and joy. Yet when the choice was offered I did not know what we could responsibly undertake, what was best for our family and the baby. I did not know how to decide.[4]

Deciding what type of child you can parent requires brutally honest soul-searching, intense prayer, and counseling from your adoption professional. The checklist isn't set in stone; you can tweak it throughout the adoption process. Your social worker (who partners with you in discerning what child will best fit your family) may veer from the checklist, as well. Don't be surprised if she asks you to consider accepting a referral for a child far outside the parameters you checked off.

The Prenatal Exam

Once you complete the checklist, you're ready for the pre-natal exam. Don't worry; the exam only lasts about three months. And don't even try to talk your way out of it—all prospective parents must complete a home study. The term *home study* is a misnomer, because the home study does not evaluate your home; it evaluates *you.* A more apt description might be *parent study.* Similar to the pre-marital counseling required for many couples, the home study prepares you to become an adoptive parent. A social worker certified

Surprise Gifts

■ ■ ■

When Sybil Smith-Gray completed her checklist, she specified that she wanted to adopt a healthy older child. She told her social worker, "Do not attempt to place a sick and disturbed child in my home. Don't do it."

A few weeks later Sybil got a call from her social worker, who said, "I think I've found your daughter. There's just one small glitch."

Sybil held her breath, ready to read her the riot act.

Her social worker continued, "There are two children—a sibling pair. As far as we know, there are no behavior or mental-health issues, no developmental delays, and no medical concerns. They just need a family."

Now, six years later, Sybil describes her family as "happy as all get-out." Things are not perfect, she qualifies. Her girls, 9 and 10, and her birth son, 12, sometimes drive her nuts. And there are days when her kids think Mom is nuts. "But I could not have ordered a more perfect union," she insists. "Because I spoke up without shame and without fear about what I really wanted, I guess, in a way, I did order this union."

or licensed to conduct home studies gathers information about you and writes a report that summarizes her findings and evaluates your parenting fitness.

You're most likely to procure a thorough, legally-binding home study from a licensed public or private adoption agency. If you plan to adopt internationally, most countries accept only agency home studies; however, your home study can be completed by a different agency than the one that places your child. Some independent private practices also complete home studies. Before hiring them learn whether their reports include all the state-mandated elements. If they cut corners, you'll likely have to pay additional fees to fill in the gaps.

It's important that you and the social worker who handles your home study feel comfortable with one another. If your social worker is not wholeheartedly committed to helping you or you feel squeamish sharing the intimate details of your life with that person, you can request someone different. Remember, you are hiring the services of the social worker, not the other way around. If you switch social workers midstream you'll probably be out some money. But your adoption will progress more smoothly in the long run if you work with a person you like, respect, and trust.

While you're unlikely to see the report your social worker compiles about you, the findings may be shared with other agencies that are attempting to locate a child who's a good match with your family. Sometimes, information from the report is shared with prospective birth parents. If you're concerned about the confidentiality of your report, ask your social worker to limit the ways she shares your information.

I believe every prospective parent—birth or adoptive—should be required to complete a home study. In fact, home studies should be a high school graduation requirement; they might serve as a deterrent to unplanned pregnancy. Imagine the following questions on a standardized test:

1. Describe your sexual history.

2. Describe your use of alcohol, illegal drugs, and/or prescription medications.

3. Describe your typical weekend activities.

4. Describe your relationships with your parents and your siblings.

5. Describe experiences that contributed to your emotional growth and maturity.

6. Describe your past and present religious practices.

7. Describe your educational background and work history. What are your career plans after you have a child?

8. Describe the type of home environment you can provide for a child.

9. Describe the methods of discipline you will use as a parent.

10. Describe your greatest strengths and weaknesses as a future parent.

The dozens of questions you answer can be summed up in a sentence: "Explain everything about your private life, your family, your hopes and dreams, and your opinions on every subject you can think of."

And that's just the beginning. Similar to someone who's applying to be an FBI agent, you'll undergo a criminal and child abuse background check (which includes fingerprinting), a physical exam by a doctor, and a home inspection. You'll provide copies of birth certificates; marriage licenses and divorce decrees (if applicable); financial statements that verify your income and report your savings, investments, insurance policies, and debts. And you'll solicit letters of reference from friends, co-workers, supervisors, clergy, and extended family members.

Your social worker will interview you several times. Her goal is to get to know you and to help you work through any issues of concern. If you are married, your social worker may conduct both individual and joint interviews. If you have other children, your social worker might interview them, as well.

Behind Closed Drawers

Your social worker will also visit your home—both pre- and post-adoption—to examine its safety and suitability for a child. During our preplacement home visit, the social worker peeked in the cupboard under our kitchen sink to see whether cleanser, dishwashing soap, and roach killer were stored within reach of toddlers. She asked if we had any loaded firearms lying around. She verified that our smoke detectors and fire extinguishers were up to code. She recommended installing safety gates across the stairway. She checked out the room where our future child would sleep. She scoped out our yard and met our pets. And she watched as one of the neighbor kids skated down our driveway and smashed into our garage door.

She did not put on white gloves and run her index finger over our furniture. Despite the effort we had put into scouring our home top to bottom, our social worker did not expect our abode to be dressed for a *Better Homes and Gardens* photo shoot. In fact, she said she preferred the homey, "lived-in" feel.

Scrappin' Your Life

The final portion of the home study is an autobiographical profile. Essentially, the profile is your life story. Culling from your responses to the myriad questions you've already answered, you bare your soul one final time in an explosion of words that shouts, "Please love me!"

If you're planning a domestic adoption in which pregnant women choose the parents for their child, you'll also prepare an autobiographical scrapbook (commonly called a *portfolio*) that will be shared with prospective birth parents. The pregnant parents who look at your portfolio won't be unduly concerned with your grammar and punctuation. They want to know whether they can connect with you emotionally and whether they can trust you to provide a safe, loving home for their child. They will, however, decide whether they want to meet you based solely on the information in your portfolio.

Some prospective birth parents read dozens of profiles, and like human resource managers, decide who makes the cut after reading only the first paragraph of each. The people who liked our portfolio, for instance, said they were attracted to us because we mentioned our favorite books (The Lord of the Rings trilogy), favorite movie *(The Sound of Music)*, favorite pet (golden retriever), and careers (high-school teachers) early in the letter.

When you write your letter, avoid flowery prose about the pregnant woman's "situation." Since your profile is a generic letter, you don't know the details of a particular woman's situation. Most women who are planning to release a child for adoption don't want to be coddled or pitied while they're trying to make a thoughtful, rational decision. Their main concern is getting to know *you*.

Your letter should present a balanced overview of your life, and can include the following:

- concrete details and anecdotes about your passions, your faith, your favorite things, your hobbies, your hopes and dreams
- a brief, non-cheesy explanation of why you want to adopt
- a description of your parenting style and your views on discipline
- if applicable, an explanation of your comfort level with open adoption
- if you're married, a discussion of how you met, how you fell in love, and the current "state of the union"
- if you're single, an explanation of your history and a description of the resources available to help you be an effective single parent

Be aware that the baby's father, parents of the pregnant woman, and additional "significant others" may read your profile. Include information that will interest both female and male readers. Keep in mind that some pregnant parents are offended by the term "birth parent." Rather than beginning your letter with "Dear Birth Parent," it might be wise to open with a generic salutation: "Hi."

Try not to get discouraged if you don't receive an instant positive response to your portfolio. It doesn't mean there's something wrong with you. While one pregnant woman might toss your letter over her shoulder, another will think it's perfect. Prayerfully write your letter, and then release it in joyful anticipation that God will put it into the hands of the people for whom He intends it.

Showers of Blessings

As you journey to adoption, you'll crave support from others who care about you. The operative word here is *support.* Not *advice*—you'll get plenty of that from your adoption social worker. But, like all expectant parents, you hope your impending parenthood will be acknowledged. You hope your loved ones will joyfully anticipate the homecoming of your new child.

If your extended family and friends don't seem to be taking much notice of your "pregnancy," it's not because they don't care; it's because they aren't sure what to say or do. Some supporters, on the other hand, go overboard in their enthusiasm. They drive you crazy, demanding updates on a daily (or hourly) basis.

Regardless of whether new developments materialize, keep your supporters informed. Regular updates emotionally prepare your supporters for your child's arrival and assure them they're participating with you in the adoption.

During the wait for your child, concentrate on eating right, exercising, and getting some recreation. Invite your supporters to accompany you to the movies, the mall, the beach, a restaurant, or to join you at the ski slope, on a bike ride, or for a walk. Keeping active will help you avoid obsessing about your pending parenthood.

One critical fact your loved ones need to understand is that your child's homecoming is not necessarily a permanent one. For many parents, the days and weeks immediately following a child's arrival are the most stressful of the entire adoption process. In domestic adoptions, for instance, birth parents who have relinquished parental rights are granted a grace period—ranging from 48 hours to six months, depending on the state—during which they can change their minds. Parents who plan to adopt a foster child often wait months—even years—for court proceedings that may or may not grant them permanent custody. Parents who adopt internationally may wait anxiously for a diagnosis concerning their medically fragile child. Despite the uncertainty surrounding a child's homecoming, it's imperative that your supporters welcome your child's home-coming with the same enthusiasm they would celebrate the birth of a much-anticipated baby.

Help your supporters understand that your "labor" and "delivery" may occur quickly and unexpectedly, and that when it happens, you'll be grateful for all the help you can get. Robert and I brought our son home only four days after learning we would become his parents. Our journey to meet him included two full days of driving followed by a nine-hour plane flight. We were thrilled when my brother and his wife offered to accompany us to the foster home to share in the "birth" of our son into our family.

During our first weeks of parenthood, we relied on gracious rela-tives who lent us a car seat, crib, and other infant essentials. When friends delivered casseroles and gifts, offered to babysit, and *oohed* and *aahed* over our baby, their enthusiasm honored the legitimacy of our new little family.

You may prefer to wait until immediately before or soon after your child's arrival to decorate your child's room and to purchase clothing and other necessities. Because your child's arrival date is unpredict-able, you might feel reluctant to get your hopes up, fearful of having them dashed by an unexpected glitch. But your friends don't know that. Their feelings will be hurt if you decline their offer to throw you a shower. Tell them you'd be delighted if they'd schedule a shower—after your child comes home. Then explain why.

Perhaps the most important way you can nurture your family's long-term health is to join your local adoption community. You'll find other adoptive parents at regional support groups, at church, at adoption agencies, and on the Internet. Connecting with others

The Chaos Theory

■ ■ ■

When Robert and I worked on our home study, I reveled in the research, writing, and revision. I loved expounding about the merits of our beautiful home, our loyal dog, and our fulfilling careers. The paperwork represented the only aspect of the adoption process I felt I could control. The rest of the process was chaotic. I felt as if the bottom had dropped out of my life, and I wondered whether things would ever be "normal" again.

Searching for encouragement, I turned to Scripture and discovered Jeremiah, an Old Testament prophet who ministered during the reigns of Judah's last five kings. Jeremiah's life was chaotic, to put it mildly. As he unswervingly proclaimed God's judgment against the unfaithful kingdom of Judah, Jeremiah was ignored, sneered at, persecuted, threatened, accused of treason, and deported.

Tempted to resign his job as God's spokesman, Jeremiah alternately complained about his difficult life and praised God for standing by him through the tough times. But he allowed God to reshape him during the midst of the chaos. And as he did, Jeremiah developed endurance.

As you labor to bring your child home, you too may feel alternately peeved at God and thankful for the privilege of enlarging your family through adoption. Invite God to restore order from the chaos that reigns during the adoption process. Soak up encouragement from the apostle Paul, who encourages you to "pray all the time...don't quit in hard times...thank God no matter what happens."[5] No matter how bruised your feet may get along the path to parenting, God promises that as you exercise your faith, He will accompany you on the journey.

who understand the unique aspects of adoption helps dispel the iso-
lation you'll sometimes feel.

■ ■ ■

Adopting is painful labor—labor that etches permanent stretch
marks onto your heart. As you look for wisdom during the conception, pregnancy, labor, and delivery of your child, God promises to
give it generously. God urges you to view this time as an opportunity to grow closer to Him. He'll help you see where you're going as
you journey to adoption; His words throw a beam of light on your
path and broaden the path beneath your feet, so your ankles don't
turn.[6] When you trust God to guide you on the path to adoption,
"The Dreaded Home Study" doesn't seem so dreaded after all. In
fact, it seems more like a labor of love.

5

Missed Conception

5

Adopt and You'll Get Pregnant?

The day Robert and I brought home our first child, we took a ferry across Washington State's Puget Sound from Bainbridge Island to Seattle. Two female passengers—one of them pregnant—observed me carrying our newborn son. "How old is he?" they inquired.

"Six days," I announced proudly.

Like guided missiles, two pairs of eyes homed in on my slender midsection.

"You look incredible!" gasped the pregnant woman. "How'd you get so thin so soon after giving birth?"

"I didn't give birth to him, but I've been expecting him for five years."

"First Comes Love, Next Comes Marriage, Then Comes the Baby in a Baby Carriage"

From the time I was a young girl I had a Master Plan. I assumed someday I'd find Mr. Right, marry him, and have his babies. I did meet Mr. Right and marry him. Our newlywed Master Plan included establishing careers as high-school teachers, attending grad school, seeing as much of the world as possible, and purchasing a home. Robert, a math teacher who creates convoluted budgets "just for fun," estimated we would be financially ready to have children after five years of marriage.

So, after five years of wedded bliss, we got to work on Project: Baby. With our graduate studies complete, Robert and I had our summers off to travel and relax (I'd heard that relaxing helps you get pregnant). We traveled to Great Britain. No baby. We traveled to Australia. No baby. We traveled to France. No baby. We traveled to Scandinavia. Still no baby.

My sisters-in-law, who never traveled, were breeding babies as quickly as rabbits. Robert's brother informed us that all he had to do was look at his wife and she got pregnant. Maybe that was the problem. We just weren't doing it right.

It seemed as if everyone but us was either pregnant or had a baby. It seemed as if our Master Plan—or my ovaries, or Robert's sperm— was malfunctioning. "Why is this happening to us?" we questioned. This kind of stuff wasn't supposed to plague healthy, well-educated, financially secure, churchgoing married couples who were anxious to become parents.

Robert and I did what any healthy, well-educated, financially secure, churchgoing couple would do in our position: We cried. We fretted. We begged God for a baby. And we visited the doctor. And then we visited an infertility specialist. We spent lots of time with our specialist. So much time, in fact, that he began to feel like one of the family.

Meanwhile, our high-school students were beginning to wonder about us. Year after year my ever-so-tactful female students inquired, "Do you have children? Why not? Don't you like kids? When are you going to get pregnant? You'll look sooo cute when you're pregnant!"

My in-laws demanded additional grandchildren and our friends offered heaps of unsolicited advice about how to achieve pregnancy: *Just get busy! Stand on your head—it worked for me. Stay out of hot tubs. Change your diet. Pray harder. Relax.*

The endless battery of poking, prodding tests produced no definitive diagnosis to our dilemma. But even if the tests had indicated one or the other of us was "to blame," Robert and I agreed we were in this together. If one of us was infertile, we both were. We began a discussion that would alter the course of our Master Plan:

- Does our inability to conceive a child make me less womanly or manly?

- How important is it to carry on the family genes through a biological child?

- How crucial is it to experience pregnancy and child-birth?

- Are we willing to spend our life savings—and then some—to pursue medical treatment that offers no guarantee of becoming pregnant?

Plan B

During the time we were weighing these questions, several of our friends adopted. Intrigued, Robert and I closely followed their progress. As we peppered our friends with questions and celebrated their children's homecoming, we began to warm to adoption. Three main factors—finances, physicians, and philosophy—cemented our decision to adopt a child.

Finances. In the days before the Federal Adoption Tax Credit, very few financial incentives for adoption existed. And because our health insurance didn't cover fertility treatment, Robert and I knew we wouldn't be able to afford both treatment and adoption. For us, it was an either/or choice.

Physicians. As our fertility specialist explained the gamut of tests and treatments, I felt a tad squeamish. The tests I'd already undergone ranged from uncomfortable to downright painful. I don't like pain. During one procedure, my doctor kindly informed me, "The tests get more painful from here on. If you're strongly considering adoption, now would be a good time to stop the infertility workups." I took his advice to heart.

Philosophy. Infertility shredded our Master Plan and forced us to discard our assumptions about how we would achieve parenthood. It all boiled down to one pivotal question: *Do we want to be pregnant—or do we want to be parents?*

Pregnancy meant rejoicing at the first flutter of tiny feet kicking inside me. It meant squinting at ultrasound pictures of our baby, trying to identify body parts. It meant basking in the admiration of those who'd inquire, "How far along are you?" But pregnancy represents only the first nine months of parenting whereas the rest of the journey lasts a lifetime. We chose parenthood.

Mourning Sickness

Before we pursued adoptive parenthood, Robert and I allowed ourselves to mourn the death of our dream for biological parenthood. Our grieving was private. Few people offered condolences. There was no memorial service…no one for whom to mourn. We grieved the loss of babies who never existed—of babies who would never exist.

For many infertile couples, adjusting to the idea of adoption is a lengthy process. Henry and Jennifer Laible tried "just about everything"—from timed intercourse to fertility drugs to intrauterine insemination to in vitro fertilization—during the seven years they underwent fertility treatment. After several rounds of treatment, Henry and Jennifer looked into domestic adoption but didn't feel motivated to begin the paperwork.

Meanwhile, their doctors informed them they were perfect candidates for in vitro fertilization (IVF). Jennifer and Henry tried IVF and became pregnant with twins, but lost the twins ten weeks into the pregnancy.

After seven years of failed treatments Jennifer and Henry admitted to one another, "This is not working. This is not the way we're going to build our family."

For three months they quietly grieved. "We stepped back into a normal life and got to know each other again without the presence of drugs or a doctor," says Jennifer. She spent the summer doing "gardening therapy," tugging dead grass out of her lawn with a pitchfork and "whaling on each piece of grass till all the dirt came out." Then she planted flowers and shrubs and watched them grow. "I needed to see something grow—I needed a healthy way to channel my energy and my grief," she explains.

The couple also frequented the Internet, investigating adoption agencies and programs. At the end of the summer, Jennifer and Henry decided to move on. "Even though we felt sad about our infertility, we felt peaceful, as if God was closing the door and saying, 'Don't go back there.' We had no desire to consider infertility treatment again."

Instead, a new dream stirred within Jennifer and Henry: the desire to adopt a child from Guatemala. "We had always talked about adoption, and once we decided to do it we jumped in with both feet," says Jennifer. She and Henry viewed the home-study paperwork as a marriage enrichment activity. "We spent a full weekend working individually on our essays and then shared what we had written during a special dinner. We blitzed our dossier paperwork; we were so eager to get it done." Six months later, the new parents traveled to Guatemala to bring home their first child.

Infertility Management 101

Giving up the dream of biological parenthood to pursue adoption requires eagerness to exchange puking for paperwork, weight gain for wait time, obstetricians for adopticians, epidurals for referrals, and vaginal delivery for special delivery. Robert and I made the transition quickly, replacing the dashed hopes infertility wrought with high hopes to adopt. But I still experienced occasional twinges of longing for a birth child. When I saw pregnant women, jolts of jealousy coursed through me. When friends discussed childbirth, a shadow of sadness crept over me. I had assumed that my commitment to building a family through adoption would put those feelings to rest. I had assumed we had resolved our infertility.

Then it hit me. Infertility is a chronic medical condition, one that requires management over the course of a lifetime. I needed to focus less on *resolving* my infertility and more on *managing* it. Managing infertility means admitting it wounds me—physically, emotionally, and spiritually. Managing infertility means I can expect old wounds to rip open when I attend baby showers or watch a mother nurse her child. Managing infertility means allowing myself to wonder what it would be like to have a child with Robert's blue eyes and my thick hair; a child who mimics Robert's habit of misplacing keys or my obsession with cleaning house when I'm stressed. Managing infertility means accepting the fact that, while my desire for a birth child has diminished, it will never entirely disappear.

Spiritual Crisis

Managing infertility also means acknowledging the spiritual crisis it precipitates. During the years Robert and I tried to conceive, we confronted God: "Why do so many of our students get pregnant unintentionally when we want to be pregnant more than anything in the world, and can't? Don't you want us to be parents, God?"

Furious at God for His silence and seeming passivity, I felt tempted to abandon my faith. Yet I simultaneously reached for God, yearning for His comfort and hoping against hope He heard my prayers and would answer.

A single Bible verse wreaked havoc with my spirit—Genesis 1:28. Immediately after God created Adam and Eve, He blessed them, saying, "Be fruitful, and multiply, and fill the earth." Since Adam and Eve were the first humans, there obviously weren't any children hanging around for them to adopt; they had no choice but to pro-create the old-fashioned way.

Throughout the course of history people have taken this passage to heart, maintaining it's their Christian duty to bear children. But what about those of us who can't increase the world's population through traditional means? Does God intend that we not enjoy the privilege of parenting?

Misconceived Advice

My spiritual quandary intensified when others piously advised, "God must be trying to teach you a lesson. You probably have unconfessed sin in your life. God will bless you with a child when you are completely in His will."

When people pointed out I wasn't pregnant because of some secret or long-forgotten sin I had neglected to confess, I'd seethe inside and mentally respond, *The only unconfessed sin I must beg for-giveness for is the black eye I just contemplated giving you.*

Instead, I'd blithely reply, "If God blessed only those who are completely in His will, would any of us have children?"

Sandra Glahn, author of *When Empty Arms Become a Heavy Burden* and *The Infertility Companion,* told me about an experience she had when she was the guest on a live radio call-in show. "A pastor phoned to say that during his ministry career, 19 couples had confided in him about their infertility troubles. He said that the 17 couples who repented of the sin in their lives conceived; the other two couples had obviously refused to repent, because they remained childless."

The show's host—a professional counselor—quickly alerted the listening audience that the pastor had shared a common misconception about infertility. Sandra, in turn, explained the errant theology linking infertility with sin, a topic she addresses thoroughly in her book, *The Infertility Companion.*

All who live under the banner of God's love can rest assured that fertility challenges are not God's punishment for sin. Jesus sacrificed His life so that those who confess their sins and accept Him as their savior receive complete, irrevocable forgiveness for every sin they have ever committed. Most amazingly, God not only forgives,

Taking Your Case to God

■ ■ ■

One of my Old Testament heroes—Job—could have written a book instructing people in crisis. A wealthy, influential man, Job was devoted to God. But he experienced a crisis of nightmarish proportions: Bolts of lightning burned his 7000 head of sheep (and their shepherds) to a crisp. Then a tornado killed his seven sons and three daughters. Finally, Job's entire body erupted in painful, oozy sores.

Three of Job's buddies heard about his trouble and showed up to "keep him company and comfort him."[1] For seven days and nights they sat with him in silence. Finally, Job broke his silence and cursed his fate. Job's horrified friends concluded that his suffering was a result of some sin he'd committed, and for the next 33 chapters, they unrelentingly chastised Job and urged him to repent, saying, "Do genuinely upright people ever lose in the end?...if you scrub your hands of sin...you'll forget your troubles...full of hope, you'll relax, confident again."[2]

Fed up with the incessant attacks from his so-called friends, Job took his case directly to God, telling Him "My complaining to high heaven is bitter, but honest."[3] Job refused to blame God for his sorry state; he simply brought his disappointment to God.

God responded by taking Job on a whirlwind tour of creation, pointing out the scope of His rule and control as Creator. At the end of the tour, a humbled yet awed Job told God, "I'm convinced: You can do anything and everything. Nothing and no one can upset your plans."[4]

but forgets our sin. Though we do suffer consequences from sins we have committed, God does not use forgiven sins as an excuse to punish us.

Human nature hasn't changed much since Job (see the sidebar) tagged his friends "a bunch of miserable comforters." In the introduction to the book of Job in *The Message* paraphrase, Eugene Peterson writes, "Sufferers attract fixers the way roadkills attract vultures." Armed with just enough biblical knowledge to be dangerous, "fixers" dole out spiritual diagnosis and prescription to infertile couples.

In the book *Hope When You're Hurting*, Larry Crabb and Dan Allender explain that people who feel powerless respond in a variety of ways to people with problems:[5]

- *They attack.* "Why are you so upset about not being able to get pregnant? If you think parenting is such a cakewalk, you can have one of my kids."

- *They moralize.* "I warned you that you waited too long before trying to get pregnant. Now you're too old and your reproductive organs are shriveled. If you would have started trying when you were in your 20s, you wouldn't be having this problem."

- *They spiritually mumble.* "Maybe God thinks you're not ready to be a parent. But He'll help if you ask Him. God works for the good of those who love Him, and all that. You just need to pray harder and have faith."

- *They practice amateur therapy.* "So, what do you think got you into this predicament? How do you feel about it? What are you afraid to tell me?"

- *They give good old-fashioned advice.* "You need to work in the church nursery. Your hormones will respond positively to holding the newborns and you'll be more likely to conceive."

"Gospel communities don't repair people, they nourish them," write Crabb and Allender. When voices that purport to proclaim

God's Word cut you down, turn them off. Instead, listen to the Voice that assures you of your infinite worth: The Lord's voice. Like Job, you can choose to maintain your faith. When you take your shattered dreams directly to God, you, like Job, place your feet in God's footprints.[6] The Creator of the universe is durable. God is a place of refuge—He helps you battle the enemies of disappointment, anger, and heartache.

"The Lord Is Close to the Brokenhearted"

Robin Chukitus discovered God's character as she battled the familiar enemies of disappointment, anger, and heartache. "From the time I was very young, I looked forward to becoming a mother," she says. Robin married at 19 and within a few years, she and her husband, Drew, began trying to get pregnant. Each passing month Robin received a subtle reminder that she needed to remain patient. "Surely God will bless me," she thought.

Months turned into years—five years, then ten, then fifteen— and each year Robin's frantic depression and anger at God increased. She could focus on nothing but her infertility. "I gazed toward heaven and cried, 'God, where are You?' I prayed He would take away my desire to be a mother. I blamed Him for withholding blessing from me."

Robin concedes that pain, sorrow, and grief became her god. Instead of running *to* God for comfort and love, she ran *away* from Him. "In essence, I placed myself on the throne by trying to plan my future and demanding God bless it rather than understanding God's true purpose for my life and being blessed in the midst of that."

As she raged at God, Robin remembered the words of Psalm 34:18: "The LORD is close to the brokenhearted and saves those who are crushed in spirit." She decided to bring her disappointment to God, acknowledging that only God could mend her broken heart. "It was time to surrender my infertility to God's incredible love," she says.

Robin chose to believe the words of the apostle Peter, who urged, "Cast all your anxiety on him because he cares for you."[7] She prayed, "Lord, You know what's best for me. I want to trust You." As she laid aside her agenda, Robin's depression, sorrow, and bitterness melted. Nineteen years after her first attempt to become pregnant, God blessed Robin and Drew through the adoption of their son, Ian.

Robin reminds me of Hannah, an infertile woman who risked intimacy with God.[8] From the desolation of her soul, Hannah cried out to God, weeping bitterly as she laid her anguish at His feet. Both Hannah—and Robin—turned to God even in their stubbornness, trusting that God would understand their pain. They invited God to enter into the darkest moments of their lives with them.

Jesus has the eyes of a person who knows His way about the ruins in our lives, writes the twentieth-century German theologian Helmut Thielicke.

> He became one of the wounded because he wanted to be one of us. And therefore that Face does not vanish when the candles go out. Here is One who is waiting and looking for me.[9]

Jesus finds us in the midst of our despair and offers comfort. He extends His hand to those whose bodies, minds, and spirits are worn out and invites, "Come to me. Get away with me and you'll recover your life. I'll show you how to take a real rest."[10]

While the reasons for our fertility impairment may not become clear to us during our lifetime, God promises that those who remain faithful to Him won't despair forever. As we sincerely depend on Him, He wipes away our tears, He transforms our wild lament into whirling dance, and He replaces our moans of despair with songs of everlasting joy.[11]

For Jennifer and Henry Laible, the despair was replaced with the big brown eyes of their son Diego, whom they adopted from Guatemala. "I believe with all my heart that God allowed our infertility challenges and pregnancy-loss heartbreaks to prepare us to be the mommy and daddy of the children He created for us, in a country we had never thought of, and on a schedule we didn't understand," says Jennifer. "When I wipe the graham cracker and slobber paste off my shoulder and look at the sticky child who just ran up to hug me, I really am content."

Spontaneous Conception

As Robert and I moved toward adoption, we allowed hope to germinate while we simultaneously guarded our hearts against disappointment. We'd heard our share of adoption horror stories and knew adoption presented its own set of complications. But we felt prepared and excited to pour our emotional energy into pursuing a new dream.

Unaware that Robert and I had worked through our infertility issues, our friends and family seemed determined that we hold fast to our former quest of biological parenthood. "Adopt and you'll get pregnant," they advised.

When future grandparents made this comment, I suspected they were grieving over the lost opportunity to have a biological grandchild. *They probably feel guilty about our inability to get pregnant,* I realized. *Maybe they believe they unwittingly passed on defective fertility genes to Robert or me.*

While we all know people who've adopted and instantly gotten pregnant, it's not a statistical likelihood. Only 5 percent of infertile couples who adopt a child conceive spontaneously—the same percentage as infertile couples who do not adopt. My hunch is that the *adopt-and-you'll-get-pregnant* contingent sincerely believes they're advocating on our behalf. They want the best for us, and in their minds, getting pregnant is what's best for us.

We must gently educate advice-givers, explaining we chose adoption not for the faint hope of the child we might birth later but for the sake of the child we're welcoming into our family now. Adoption is not a cure for infertility. It is not a consolation prize we accept in order to achieve the ultimate goal of pregnancy. Adoption is the grand prize.

Get Pregnant, and You'll Get Pregnant

Some couples have no trouble getting pregnant and giving birth once, but when they attempt to conceive again, they experience secondary infertility. Secondary infertility is the inability to conceive or carry a pregnancy to term following the birth of one or more children. Couples with secondary infertility suffer the same emotional trauma as those with primary infertility. Their situation is compounded by a pervasive lack of sympathy from just about everyone.

Friends and family members, unaware of the couple's fertility issues, advise, "Your biological clock is ticking. You'd better get cracking on the next baby before it's too late."

If the couple decides to adopt, they're criticized by people with primary infertility, who view them as opportunistic predators for the same child they hope to adopt. "You already have a child," they accuse. "Why don't you count your blessings and enjoy the one you have?"

To further complicate matters, couples with secondary infertility wonder whether they'll be able to love their adopted child as much as they love their birth child. But the love a parent has for each of his or her children can't be measured or compared, write Debby Peoples and Harriette Rovner Ferguson in *Experiencing Infertility*. You don't have to divide your emotions equally between children as if you're slicing up a pie. "You can love each child as an individual, for who that child is and what he or she means to you. One child does not take you away from the other."[12]

Eyes Wide Open

Infertility drains those who experience it. And the stressors that accompany adoption can blindside an already fragile infertile couple. But if you enter adoption with your eyes open to the unique challenges it presents, you'll discover that the process strengthens, rather than weakens, your marriage.

If you and your spouse are currently moving from infertility to adoption, consider trying these relationship-building activities:

Institute the "five-minute rule." On a daily basis, share your feelings with one another for five minutes each. Don't try to problem-solve. Simply give one another undivided attention and share what's on your heart. Talk about things that hurt or hurtful things others say to you. Give each other permission to process your feelings about infertility and adoption differently, and at different rates.

Developing a habit of attentive listening accomplishes three purposes:

- It helps you avoid compartmentalizing your feelings about infertility and adoption.

- It helps you avoid obsessing about the issues.

- It helps you and your spouse understand each other's feelings.

Establish quiet time. Your quiet time can be an extension of your five-minute sharing time or it can be a separate period during which you sit near your spouse in quiet reflection. If you prefer, you can each create a personal space of solitude. Try to find a spot that's free from distractions, then relax and allow the clutter in your mind to dissipate as you listen for God's voice.

You may wish to journal your thoughts and prayers or to worship through singing, playing an instrument, or meditating on Scripture. Don't feel guilty if you get drowsy or fall asleep—a nap may be just what you need. Scheduling down time every week will decrease your stress level and increase your awareness of the ways in which God is working in your lives.

Share a passion. Sometimes you need a distraction from all the emotional junk that threatens to overwhelm you. Find a hobby, sport, or activity in which you share an interest. Pouring your energy into something fun recreates the sense of couple-closeness you may have lost during infertility.

■ ■ ■

The Master Plan I created as a young girl turned out extraordinarily different than what I had envisioned. I'm thankful for that, though. At times, I'm even grateful for our fertility challenges. Had it not been for infertility, Robert and I may have taken parenting for granted. Instead, we view every child as a gift and we treasure our sons as surprise packages from God. True to His promise in Psalm 113, God gives childless couples a family, and He gives us joy as the parents of children.

6

Out of Sight, Out of Mind

It's Not Easy Being a Birth Mom

My husband and I knew that someone would have to give birth to our baby. But we avoided thinking about our future child's birth mother. We preferred to envision a pregnant mystery woman who would materialize out of nowhere, place her baby into our loving arms, and then vanish, never to be heard from again.

We blissfully lived the fantasy until we got "the call" from our adoption caseworker. A young couple had chosen us as potential parents for their unborn baby. They wanted to meet us. In a flash, our fantasy birth parents materialized into real—and frightening— human beings. Teenage human beings. Teenage human beings who had the power to determine whether Robert and I would become parents.

All the qualms about birth parents that we had locked in the armored boxes of our minds exploded. *Would they be smart or stupid? From good homes or homeless? Healthy or drug addicts?*

We agreed to meet them, imagining that once the baby was ours, we'd drive our Toyota Camry into the sunset and be done with them. Sure, we'd dutifully send the required photos and update letters, but we didn't want "those people" interfering in our lives.

We arranged to meet the couple and their pregnancy counselor at a restaurant near their hometown. As Robert and I drove into the restaurant's parking lot, we warily scanned the premises. There were no teenagers in sight. We zipped to the far reaches of the parking lot and hid our sedan behind the most monstrous pickup we could find—a Ford F-350 crew cab—so they wouldn't spot our car's license plate and hunt us down.

Inside the restaurant, we met a dark-haired, dark-eyed couple named Jen and Ben. As we all nervously perused our menus, we snatched surreptitious peeks at one another. The waiter appeared, order pad in hand. His broad smile encompassed all of us. "What can I get for your family today?"

We glanced at one another, eyebrows raised. Minutes later, as the waiter strode away, Robert remarked, "I wonder which of us the waiter thinks are the mom and dad?"

It was as if Robert had popped a balloon. Our suppressed laughter burst out, dissipating the tension. Within minutes, we were chatting like old friends. We discovered that we shared common interests and outlooks on life. The waiter had been correct. We were related, in some bizarre fashion. Although we didn't fully reveal our thoughts to one another at the time, we had each come to the same realization: We would become a family.

During that meeting with our future son's birth parents, Robert and I sensed that Jen and Ben cared deeply for their unborn baby. When I asked Ben what he would want his son to know about him, Ben responded, "I want him to know I love him."

Gee, these nice kids were making it difficult for us to imagine adopting their baby and then carrying on with our lives as if they didn't exist! They were an all-American couple. They didn't do drugs. They didn't smoke. They were involved in a steady, monogamous relationship. They came from upstanding, middle-class families. They were honor-roll students. They were Christians. They were the kind of teenagers any parent would love to have around the house. Robert and I were tempted to bring them home with us. This lovely couple faced just one little issue, evident in Jen's protruding belly.

Jen and Ben had assumed the warnings about premarital sex leading to pregnancy applied to other people, not to them.

As we ate, Ben fired questions at us while Jen observed. "I wanted to not like Robert and Laura," Jen reflected later. "I was scared and envious, because they would raise my baby, and I wouldn't. But I liked them. I trusted them." On the way home from the restaurant, Jen and Ben made their decision: "Those are the parents we need for our baby."

Four days later, our son was born. His birth parents named him Benjamin Robert, after both his dads.

The Changing Face of Adoption

Very few couples make the decision Jen and Ben did. In fact, less than 1 percent of never-married American women who experience an unplanned pregnancy place their child for adoption. Today's teenagers grow up in a society that views single parenting as the norm—nearly half of them spend part of their childhood living in a single parent family.[1] It hasn't always been that way.

During the first half of the twentieth century, adoption was the solution that erased the stigma of an out-of-wedlock pregnancy. Adoption began gaining public acceptance in the 1910s and 1920s. Before that point, children were adopted by relatives after their parents died unexpectedly, or because of their economic usefulness—they functioned as indentured servants and apprentices. But in the early twentieth century, the idea of marrying for love, rather than duty, became popular. Inheriting the family fortune was no longer tantamount to ensuring one's place in society. As couples intentionally built marriage partnerships, they assumed they could also intentionally build families.

The concept of adopting by choice gained momentum, as did the practice of unwed mothers relinquishing babies. The U.S. Children's Bureau estimated 16,000 to 17,000 adoptions in 1937 and 50,000 adoptions per year by 1945.[2]

Choices in the Past

■ ■ ■

Had Jen and Ben lived in the 1950s, they may have gotten married—nearly half the unwed women who became pregnant made that choice. Marrying Ben would have legitimized Jen's pregnancy in society's eyes, even though she likely would have been kicked out of school and treated as a social outcast.

While a high percentage of teenage mothers in the '50s got married, the number of adoptions continued to rise. In 1957, for example, there were 91,000 adoptions, which represented almost 9 percent of all premarital births.[3] Adoption was viewed as a means of giving girls who had gotten "in trouble" a second chance for marriage and legitimate motherhood.

Ironically, even though adoption was widespread in the '50s and '60s, it was cloaked in secrecy. Ben would have been a helpless bystander while Jen's parents spirited her away to visit distant relatives or to live in a commercial maternity home. Jen would have had no choice about whether to relinquish her child for adoption. She would not have been allowed to see her son after giving birth, or even to learn what sex he was. She would have received no counseling and no consolation. She would have been expected to put the whole experience behind her—to act as if she'd never been pregnant.

In the 1970s and 1980s, an array of choices became available. The women's liberation movement of the late '60s and early '70s empowered women to make their own decisions. Compounded with the legalization of abortion in 1973, the feminist movement had a drastic impact on marriage and adoption practices. The number of American households consisting of married couples plummeted from 70 percent in 1970 to 52 percent in 2000.[4] Pregnant women no longer had to decide who would raise their child, but whether their child should be born.

Although teen-pregnancy rates and abortion rates have declined steadily since 1991, today's pregnant teenage women generally opt for single parenthood. Seventy-nine percent of today's births to teenagers age 15 to 19 are nonmarital, compared to 67 percent in 1990, 48 percent in 1980, 30 percent in 1970, and 15 percent in 1960.[5] Unwed motherhood is accepted—even revered by many—while adoption is often considered a shameful option for a woman experiencing an unplanned pregnancy.

A Birth Mom's Story

When Jen and Ben learned they were pregnant, they felt determined to parent their baby. During her fifth month of pregnancy, 17-year-old Jen journaled,

> My plan is to keep the baby, of course. As soon as the baby's born I'm moving out of my house and in with Ben's family. We'll stay there till I'm stable and I (possibly we: Ben and I), can afford to rent an apartment.

During her pre-pregnancy days, Jen's classmates dubbed her "sweet little Miss Innocent." Her peers respected her for her Christian morals and ethics. She functioned as counselor and advice-giver to friends. But once they learned she was pregnant, her classmates ostracized her. Even her relationship with her best girlfriend became strained. Jen's best friend told her, "Pregnancy happens to *those* people. It doesn't happen to your best friend."

As Jen's friendships disintegrated, so did her family structure. At church services, people made spoken and unspoken accusations against Jen and her parents: *Premarital sex is a terrible sin. What kind of parents "let" their daughter get pregnant? Jen created this problem; she needs to take responsibility. If she really loves her baby, she will raise it.*

Jen's youth-group friends, unsure of how to act around a Christian girl who showed up pregnant at church, ignored her. Embarrassed and guilt-ridden, Jen and her family withdrew from their church and from one another. Jen's mother asked her to move out, and Jen spent the final four months of her pregnancy living with various friends and relatives.

Ben, who at first had seemed enthusiastic about raising their child together, began having second thoughts. He approached Jen and asked, "What do you think about adoption?"

Jen stared at him as if he was crazy. "I'm this baby's mother. How could I ever consider giving him away?" she demanded.

Even with her life falling apart around her, pregnancy was the most invigorating experience of Jen's young life. "I loved the idea that there was a little bitty baby growing inside me. I loved that I was taking care of him. That he could hear me. Every night, I'd sing him a little lullaby. I'd talk to him. I was always rubbing my belly. It was a real personal relationship."

Jen also craved the attention she received from people at school who'd approach her, rub her belly, and say, "Hi, baby."

But for Ben, the thought of raising a child at age 16 was terrifying. "I think we should look into adoption," he persisted.

Jen felt torn. She wanted to be a good mother, yet she also aspired to attend college and become a paralegal. She took stock of her circumstances. She and Ben still had a couple of years of high school left. She was on welfare. She had no job, no car, no money, and no permanent place to live. Her relationship with Ben was crumbling under the stress; deep inside, Jen admitted it was not going to last. She sensed that in their present circumstances, neither she nor Ben could provide their baby with the kind of life they wanted him to have.

Every night before falling asleep, Jen begged God for strength and courage to make it through the next day. As she prayed, she sensed God leading her towards adoption. Still, she had misgivings: *How can we give our baby away to total strangers? Will our child hate us and think we didn't want him? Will we regret this decision for the rest of our lives?*

But as Jen continued opening her mind to adoption, she noticed positive changes beginning to take place. She and Ben, who had been estranged off and on during her pregnancy, began talking with one another again. Jen felt at peace. "I thought God was trying to tell me that keeping my baby was not what He wanted me to do," she says.

Jen began exploring adoption, confident God would take care of her and her baby. "It was God who brought me to my decision. It was God who got me through the adoption process. And it was God who constantly reminded me that placing my son for adoption was not really my decision…it was His plan."

Jen says she ultimately chose adoption because of her love for the two most important people in her life at the time: her boyfriend and her unborn son. She journaled:

> I thought that all I needed to be a good parent was love. But while you do need love to parent a child, you can't parent simply with love. It's really important to me that Ben is happy. And because I love this baby so incredibly, I want him to have the best life he possibly can. I want him to have a mom and dad—a *stable* mom and dad. I want to give him a chance to have a better life than what I have to offer.

Rethinking Birth Parents

After Robert and I met Jen and Ben, we began to rethink our stereotypes about birth parents. Where was the promiscuous, desperate, HIV-positive woman we had half-expected to meet? And the baby's father…wasn't he supposed to drop out of sight the minute he discovered his girlfriend was pregnant, never to be heard from again?

Granted, some birth parents are drug addicts and prostitutes, but many of them are what we'd call "good kids"—people like Jen and Ben, who thought, *It can't happen to me.*

Statistics show that women who choose adoption generally have an unstable or nonexistent relationship with the child's father. Or, like Jen and Ben, they agree they're not ready to become parents together. Many come from noncohesive families or from homes where there's a history of alcohol abuse. Women who choose adoption often know someone else who has placed a child for adoption. They are apt to be from middle-class families, to have mothers who have completed at least one year of college, to attend religious services regularly, and to have high educational goals. They usually delay marriage and a second pregnancy longer than their counterparts who decide to parent. Twelve months after giving birth, women who choose adoption are usually employed, and they are less likely to receive public assistance than their parenting peers.[6]

Teen mothers, on the other hand, are less likely to graduate from high school or to attend college. One-third of them become pregnant again within two years of giving birth to their first child.[7]

Jen admits there was an element of selfishness in her decision to place her baby for adoption. "I *did* want to go to college and pursue a career," she says. But she and Ben didn't choose adoption to walk away from the responsibility of parenting. They chose adoption because parenting was so important to them that they wanted to be parents at the right time, with the right partner. They considered their unborn child and his future, separate from themselves and their own needs. Like any good parents, they sought to discern what was best for their child.

Jen says she's always felt content with her decision. She did become a paralegal, and she later married and gave birth to more children. Still, the birth of her first child was bittersweet joy. In the weeks following baby Ben's birth and adoption, Jen penned the following poem:[8]

If Only They Could See—If Only They Knew

Smiling broadly as I talk of him
My face alive with a joy that's rare
Friends marvel, say I'm doing so well
Others think I'm cold-hearted and that I don't care

If only they could see—if only they knew

If only they could see inside my heart
Be a part of the sadness and the pain
If only they knew of the tears I cry
Upon my pillow they leave a stain

A wonderful couple I gave him to
I know he is happy and that he is loved
The world thinks what I did was wrong
Many say I have sinned to the One above

If only they could see—if only they knew

If only they could see how much I love him
That I think of him constantly, miss him even more
If only they knew how important he is to me
And that it is me, and not him, that I abhor

I gave my son up for adoption
A son who I love more than anything
The world has no right to judge or to offer opinions
For the world does not see,
Does not know what's inside of me

A Birth Mother's Love

A mom whose story is told in the Bible helps us understand the anguish birth mothers feel as they plan for their child's future and then let go of the little person they gave birth to and love deeply.

Moses' birth mother, Jochebed, an Israelite, makes an adoption plan for her infant son when the king of Egypt institutes his version of ethnic cleansing. As recorded in the book of Exodus, Pharaoh decides the Israelites are "too numerous." He fears that if war breaks out, the Israelites will join his enemies (a shrewd assumption, particularly since this ruthless king oppressed the Israelites with forced labor). Pharaoh orders his people: "Every boy that is born, drown him in the Nile."[9]

About the time Pharaoh issues this edict, Moses is born to Jochebed and her husband, Amram. They hide their son from the Egyptians for three months. Then, fearing for Moses' life, Jochebed places her baby in a watertight basket and puts it to float among the reeds along the bank of the Nile. She stations her young daughter Miriam as a lookout.

Pharaoh's grown daughter discovers the babe, takes pity on him, and decides to adopt him as her own. When Miriam approaches with a suggestion, Pharaoh's daughter agrees to hire Jochebed to nurse the infant.

The culminating moment in Moses' adoption comes in Exodus 2:10, after he is weaned. His birth mother delivers him to Pharaoh's daughter, and he officially becomes the son of the Egyptian princess.

Jochebed exhibited incredible strength of character in weaving her intricate adoption plan for Moses. She essentially chose his adoptive family by placing the basket near the spot she knew Pharaoh's daughter would come to bathe. Perhaps Jochebed had heard rumors of the princess's kindheartedness. Jochebed hoped against hope the princess's servants would coo over the baby and implore Pharaoh's daughter to rescue him.

Jochebed had no idea what God had in store for her little one, yet she trusted His gentle prompting and she released her baby into His hands. Even though she knew she was giving Moses a chance at life, Jochebed must have felt intense anguish as she tenderly placed her son in the basket and kissed him goodbye.

■ ■ ■

Jochebed's story reminds me to thank God for Jen and Ben, good parents who, during the first nine months of baby Ben's life in the womb, doted on him, delighted in him, and planned for his future. During the two days Jen spent with baby Ben in the hospital, she did what any new mom would do. She stared at her son. She memorized his features. She spent as much time as possible with him, simply watching him sleep.

Then she said goodbye. "Ben showed up and we cried together for a long time," recalls Jen. "We left baby Ben in the hospital with our adoption counselor and drove away. I cried the whole way home."

Although Jen's world had crumbled, she dwelt in God's presence, assured that "placing Ben for adoption was not really my decision… it was His plan." There has been heartache, Jen admits. "I've often wondered what it would have been like if I had kept him. But I never, ever doubted that what I did was right."

In the months following the adoption, Jen felt her Lord's continuous presence. "God stood by me and was there for me when I needed Him. His love supersedes the love any single person can offer. That's what pulled me through."

7

Adoption Miscarriage

Shattered Dreams

Two years into parenthood, Robert and I decided to embark on our second adoption. We returned to the agency from which we'd adopted Ben and updated our home study. At first, the events of adoption number two mirrored our idyllic first adoption; only a week after we'd completed our paperwork, 19-year-old Janet chose us to parent her unborn baby.

Janet's baby was due in a month, so she was eager to meet us right away. We met at a restaurant and spent several hours chatting with the lovely, soft-spoken young woman. Two weeks later, we dined together again, this time with 2-year-old Ben in attendance. Janet seemed delighted with Ben and assured us everything was a "go" for the adoption. I cautiously revealed that I had bought two outfits for the baby and that we were preparing the nursery.

The day the baby was born, our caseworker called to tell us Janet had decided to parent her child. Janet wanted us to know she felt guilty for leading us to believe we'd adopt her baby. But her family and friends had helped her find child care and had given her baby clothes, a crib, and an apartment. Janet felt she had enough resources in place to manage parenting, attending college, and working. The baby was born on my birthday. That year, instead of celebrating my birthday, I swallowed the pain of dashed hopes.

When people asked how I was doing, I shrugged nonchalantly and replied, "Just fine." *I don't deserve to grieve for this baby,* I rationalized. *He wasn't mine in the first place.*

Privately, Robert and I wondered what was wrong with us. "Did we unintentionally say something that turned Janet off?" we asked each other. "Did she see Ben and think, 'That's not so hard. I can raise a child as well as they can.' Did she disapprove of our parenting style?"

The week after our loss, as I waited in the checkout line at the grocery store, my attention was drawn to a man who stood in line behind me, nestling a squawking newborn in his arms. He gently stroked his baby's back and calmed her wails with kisses. Tears sprang to my eyes. *I should be holding my own baby today.*

■ ■ ■

A month after the birth of Janet's baby, our agency offered us an opportunity to adopt an eight-month-old girl. That situation, too, fell through the cracks. Two months later, yet another potential adoption failed to materialize. Then, a month after that, our hopes soared when we were invited to meet Mike and Lisa, teenagers whose baby was due in two weeks. Mike and Lisa wanted to interview us before deciding whether we would be the ones to parent their child.

When Mike explained he was 80 percent sure he wanted custody of the child, my stomach knotted into a tight ball. Lisa, her eyes shooting daggers at her ex-boyfriend, retorted she had no intention of allowing Mike to gain custody of the child. Then she announced that some friends of her parents had been pestering her for months to let them adopt the baby. But Lisa said she felt uncomfortable with the close proximity she'd have to her baby if her parents' friends adopted it. She liked the physical and emotional distance Robert and I represented.

Wary of Lisa and Mike's animosity towards one another, Robert and I steeled ourselves for another letdown. We were taken by surprise when, four days before Lisa's due date, our case worker told us Lisa and Mike wanted us to adopt their baby. I couldn't decide whether to shout for joy or to keep the information secret. If I shared the news, I faced the possibility I'd have to call everyone back a few days later to announce another rejection. My fears became reality when Lisa gave birth and opted to place the baby with the friends of her family.

■ ■ ■

Because our caseworker considered the "Lisa and Mike" situation high-risk, she had continued circulating our portfolio. The same day we learned Lisa and Mike had un-chosen us, we learned 19-year-old Monique had chosen us and was anxious to meet. Not only that, but Robert was offered a new job that day. God replaced our shattered dreams with the anticipation of another potential adoption and a career move.

Our first meeting with Monique was fabulous. A new Christian, she told us she believed God had allowed her to get pregnant so she could give her baby to people who otherwise couldn't have one. She said the baby's father was willing to sign relinquishment papers. *Was this woman for real?* After our recent interactions with prospective birth parents, Monique seemed like a gift from God...a gift that seemed almost too good to be true.

Monique, who was due in four months, adamantly assured us God was telling her we were the right family for her baby. She wanted a completely open adoption and invited me to accompany her to a pre-natal doctor appointment, where we watched a live ultrasound performance of "our" baby. She requested I be with her in the delivery room during the baby's birth.

Robert and I allowed hope to kindle. God seemed so present in this situation and all signs pointed to the adoption happening. We began to shop for infant clothes and think about names.

Eight weeks before her due date, Monique let us know she'd be taking a short trip from her home state of Washington to California to visit relatives. Three days after her arrival in California, the unthinkable happened: Monique gave birth prematurely. She phoned immediately to tell us the baby was in precarious health. Then for ten days we heard nothing.

Finally, Monique contacted her pregnancy counselor from the adoption agency and explained she'd been so concerned for the baby's health she could think of nothing else. She assured her counselor she planned to follow through with the adoption and welcomed us to call her at the hospital.

We called periodically but Monique didn't answer our calls, nor did she return our messages. Exactly a month after the baby's birth, we knew little more about his condition or about Monique's intentions than we had the day he was born. During that month I prayed constantly—for the baby, for Monique, and for us. Nauseous with worry, I couldn't sleep; couldn't eat. With a growing sense of dread, I suspected yet another baby was slipping out of our grasp.

Monique's Seattle-based pregnancy counselor tried unsuccessfully to contact her, as well. Finally, her counselor called a nurse at Monique's hospital, who told her the baby had gone home with Monique the previous week.

Our prayers for the baby's health had been answered, but Robert and I never got to touch him. We never heard him cry or coo. I saw him only once, as a two-dimensional image on an ultrasound monitor. Losing that child was the greatest disappointment of my life.

At a Loss for Words

As we absorbed this latest loss, Robert and I embarked on the now-familiar task of informing everyone that yet another almost-adoption had failed. Words could not adequately describe the grief we felt as we awkwardly conveyed the news.

We received a range of responses. The most common one was, "Oh."

"Oh?" What kind of compassionate, sympathetic response was that?

Others eagerly shared horror stories of friends who had adopted, and six months later were forced to return the baby to his birth parents. "At least you didn't get the baby home and have to give him back a few days or weeks or months later," they rationalized.

True. But somehow this glib response didn't alleviate our sadness.

A few people quoted statistics: "I've heard that at least half the pregnant women who plan an adoption don't follow through."[1] The statistics-quoters must have assumed we'd feel comforted, knowing we were part of a larger group of grieving would-be parents.

Some well-meaning friends, who equated adopting with buying a car, seemed convinced our current dealership was providing unreliable service. They recommended we shop around: "Why don't you switch agencies? Have you thought about hiring a lawyer? Or advertising in the newspaper?"

Others suggested we could get a bargain on a used model: "Why don't you try adopting an older child?"

They offered convenient solutions for replacing our out-of-stock baby: "Why not try international adoption? Or biracial adoption? Or special needs adoption?"

And then there were the folks who dispensed spiritual advice: "God didn't intend for you to have that baby," they'd intone solemnly. "It's better that his real mother raise him. God has the perfect baby picked out for you. Trials help build strength; this trial will teach you to rely more on God."

Some people were businesslike, giving us a brisk pat on the shoulder and a reassuring, "Everything will be all right."

Finally, there were those who acted as if our losses had never occurred. Unsure how to comfort us, they opted for the safest route and kept mum.

Adoption loss is like nothing I've ever encountered. Every time our caseworker called with a lead, my heart leapt into my throat as *this-might-be-the-one* anticipation mounted. I'd immediately squelch the feeling, warning myself, "Don't get too excited; don't get emotionally involved; guard your heart." But it was impossible *not* to get excited. As I waited for the phone to ring, hope and longing washed over me; hope that was replaced with sadness, embarrassment, and anger each time we learned that the child we had emotionally begun to bond with would never be ours. For Robert and me, each loss was a double whammy—we couldn't conceive a child and now we might not get to adopt one either.

After one of our failed attempts, a friend who sensed my anguish literally demanded that I grieve. I'll always treasure her firm, yet loving advice: "You have lost a child. You were planning for this baby just as you would have if you'd been pregnant. That child is gone now, and you need to let yourself mourn for him."

The most meaningful comfort I received was delivered in the simplest manner. A friend gave me a long hug, looked me in the eyes and said, "I don't know what to say, but I'm sorry for your loss. I'm thinking of you and praying for you."

She offered no platitudes. No advice. Just love.

Risky Business

The almost-adoptions Robert and I experienced represent one type of adoption loss. Other common scenarios include...

- A child someone hopes to adopt dies during childbirth.

- A country suddenly closes its doors to allowing adoptions, shutting out parents who have already accepted referrals to adopt a particular child.

- A child who has been matched with one family is adopted by a different family.

- A child from another country is matched with prospective parents and the child's birth mother reclaims him from the agency or orphanage located in her country.

- A dishonest doctor in another country produces a fake death certificate for a child who has been matched with adoptive parents. The doctor keeps the adoption fees and then re-enacts the same scam on other prospective parents or sells the baby to another family.

- Expectant parents who indicate they intend to relinquish suddenly disappear.

- A woman conceals her pregnancy from the baby's father, says the father has no interest in parenting, or claims she doesn't know the father's whereabouts. At some point, the father turns up and contests the adoption.

- A fraudulent birth mother or fraudulent adoption professional claims pregnancy when there is none; accepts thousands of dollars to cover fees, living expenses, and medical expenses when there is no intention of following through with the adoption; or promises a baby to several families simultaneously.

- A fraudulent adoption professional offers to provide a baby immediately upon receipt of an exorbitant amount of cash.

- An online swindler posts photos of children from other countries who are supposedly available for adoption, promising a quick adoption in exchange for cash.

- A fraudulent adoption professional promises the same child to multiple parents, collects payments from all of them, and then reneges or disappears.

- A "starving Nigerian teenager" whose parents were supposedly massacred during a war, e-mails pleas for a loving family to adopt him.

Some types of adoption loss have official, ominous-sounding names: *revocation, disruption,* and *dissolution.*

Revocation, or *reversal,* occurs when birth parents or legal guardians who have voluntarily placed their child with adoptive parents revoke their consent to the placement before the adoption is legally finalized and reclaim their child. In some states, consent is irrevocable. In others, birth parents can revoke consent only when there is clear evidence of fraud or duress. The grace period during which birth parents can revoke consent ranges from 48 hours to six months, depending on the state in which the adoption occurred.[2]

An adoption is *disrupted* when a child leaves an adoptive home before the adoption is legally finalized. Disruption occurs when the court rules that a child reunite with her birth family; when a child enters or returns to foster care; when the adoptive parents decide not to continue with the adoption; or when a child is placed with different adoptive parents. Typically, disruption rates in the United States range from 10 to 25 percent.[3]

Dissolution refers to an adoption that is voided—or dissolved—after legal finalization, resulting in the child entering or returning to foster care or being placed with new adoptive parents. Between 1 and 10 percent of completed adoptions dissolve; less than .1 percent of finalized adoptions are contested each year.[4]

The older the child, the more likely the adoption will be disrupted or dissolved. Children with behavioral and emotional needs and those who've experienced multiple foster care placements have a greater chance of experiencing a disrupted adoption.[5]

Cameron and Charlotte planned a foster adoption in which they'd adopt Shauna, a 12-year-old who was legally free for adoption. Shauna, who'd lived in foster care all her life, arrived at Cameron and Charlotte's home with "way more mental and social problems than we were led to believe she had," relates Charlotte. She'd been sexually abused and suffered from both Attention Deficit Disorder and a personality disorder. "She switched personalities from one minute to the next," says Charlotte. "One minute she acted like a 3-year-old, and the next minute she acted like a 16-year-old."

Charlotte, a former teacher, homeschooled Shauna to help her get on track with her schoolwork. But Charlotte, who faces chronic physical challenges of her own, had a difficult time caring for Shauna. Cameron helped as much as possible but was away at work all day.

Broken Promises, Broken Hearts

■ ■ ■

When almost-parents reluctantly give up the child they'd hoped to adopt, they are overcome with guilt. They feel like monsters at the prospect of breaking a promise they've made to their foster child—a promise to provide a permanent home to a child who's never had one.

Glenn and Anita parented three foster sons—all of whom had extensive special needs—for six, five, and four years, respectively. One of their sons was returned to his birth mother; another, who suffered from mental illness, was admitted to an institution; and the third experienced custody complications with his birth father.

"No matter how good a parent I tried to be, I wasn't able to solve their problems," says Anita. "I felt like I failed."

When they gave up custody of the boys, no one expressed sympathy. "Nobody considered them our children because we hadn't adopted them and we didn't give birth to them," says Anita.

Instead, friends commented, "Good riddance. Thank goodness you don't have to deal with *them* anymore."

Everone had assumed that Anita and Glenn were parenting the boys "as some kind of ministry or job." But that's not how Anita and Glenn viewed it. "We made an emotional commitment to those boys," explains Anita. "We expected to keep them forever, and we considered them ours."

As his wife became increasingly weaker, Cameron's concern deepened. Finally, Cameron and Charlotte agreed they weren't capable of caring for Shauna.

"It was the hardest decision we ever made," admits Charlotte. "We are very loyal people; once we make a commitment, we stick with it. Giving her up was totally out of character. We felt as if everybody—including us—was letting Shauna down."

While Charlotte and Cameron's family supported their decision to return Shauna to the group home in which she'd previously lived, friends weren't so understanding. "One friend told me I was a terrible person for doing this to a child," recalls Charlotte.

Processing Loss

There's no instruction manual for how to process adoption loss. Whether our child lived only in our heart or was physically present in our family for years, we ache for the child. But we're not sure how to grieve. If we squelch our sadness, we worry others will think we're callous for not showing emotion. If we cry inconsolably, we worry others will think we're overacting. We feel empty, cheated, and victimized by a system that let us down. If we have other children, we question why they, who anticipated a new brother or sister with such excitement, now have to suffer.

We're furious with God, demanding to know why God would allow our hopes to soar and then crash. One woman, who believes motherhood is one of God's callings for her life, questioned God through her tears: "I've done my part to become a mother and it isn't working out. God, if you're going to shut the door, why couldn't you have done so without making me go through all this?"

Another woman, whose baby lived with her for a week before his birth parents reclaimed him, confessed how difficult it was to attend church after losing her son. "I knew that if I didn't go back to church immediately, I wouldn't go at all." She would slip in to the service late and sit in the back. "I couldn't sing. I would sit in the pew and bawl. Loudly."

While she has accepted the fact that her son is gone, she knows she'll never experience complete closure. "I wonder where he is, what his name is, what he looks like now, and what his life is like. I wonder whether I'll ever see him again. And I pray for him." For her, all that remains of her son is a box filled with his baby book, his pacifier, and his first pair of shoes.

It's okay to be mad at God, writes Barbara Johnson in *Splashes of Joy in the Cesspools of Life:*

> When we scream in agony and rage at Him through our grief, He doesn't say, "Off to hell with you, Sister!" Instead, He patiently loves us…carries us…wraps His blanket of tenderness around us while we are balking, hissing and rebelling in every way.[6]

Anger that arises out of pain and grief is a normal emotional response to sudden, unexpected loss and shouldn't be viewed as a final commentary on our spiritual condition, writes Johnson. Vent your anger at God; He can take it, she advises. As you release your emotions, "the dawn of hope will break over the darkness of grief."[7]

The Forgiveness Factor

When our adoptions collapsed, I was not only angry with God; I was angry with the prospective birth parents. Jealous of their ability to get pregnant when I couldn't, I resented them for making me feel cynical and distrustful. I felt like suing them for breach of promise. They had selected us to adopt their babies. They had assured Robert and me repeatedly—with no prodding from us—that they were 100 percent committed to their adoption plan. When they had a change of heart, they didn't even bother to acknowledge our hurt. I felt used and discarded.

But no matter how much I hated to acknowledge it, I knew those young mothers and fathers cared deeply about their babies and wanted to do right by them. I knew that at some point, they had sincerely intended for us to adopt their baby. I knew their adoption defections had nothing to do with us and everything to do with their own life circumstances. I grudgingly admitted that if I was ever going to work through my losses, I needed to forgive them.

In the Bible, the ability to forgive others is closely linked to our willingness to ask forgiveness for our own shortcomings. Jesus repeatedly instructs His followers: "Forgive, and you will be forgiven." In the best-known prayer of all time—the Lord's Prayer—Jesus teaches us to ask God to "forgive us our sins, for we also forgive everyone who sins against us."[8]

Even though I wasn't thrilled to do so, I confessed my anger and bitterness and asked God to forgive me. My heart began to soften as I thanked God for giving Robert and me the opportunity to adopt not one, but several children. It softened further as I thanked God for the privilege of meeting those pregnant women and their partners and of being allowed a glimpse into their lives. As I forgave them, I began to develop a deeper compassion for those in crisis pregnancies who struggle to make the right choice for their child.

Forgiving those I felt had wronged me was the first step in the healing process. Time is another healer. Joe and Peggy Bentz—who developed a relationship with a pregnant woman who disappeared the day her C-section was scheduled—took time off of work following their failed adoption. "We had already cleared our schedules because we thought we were going to have a baby," says Joe.

After their prospective birth mother disappeared, Joe and Peggy weren't in any condition to go back to work. "That was both good and bad," explains Joe. "We had all this silent time that no baby was filling—time to worry, fret, and be angry."

He and Peggy decided to physically distance themselves from the emotional strain, taking a vacation to San Diego and then allowing an additional month to "think things through" before deciding on their next course of action. During that month, friends brought meals and kept them company—factors Joe attributes to helping them through their darkest moments.

In the midst of their disillusionment with God, Joe and Peggy clung to their faith, surrendering their hope for a child to God. They believed God would somehow redeem their situation, whether that meant they'd adopt a different child or learn to be content with child-free living. "Underneath the anger and frustration flowed a stream of hope," says Joe.

In the midst of their grief, Joe and Peggy trusted that the Redeemer who created them—who adopted them as His own—had not forgotten them. In the book of Isaiah (as paraphrased in *The Message*), God assures His people,

> When you're in over your head, I'll be there with you. When you're in rough waters, you will not go down. When you're between a rock and a hard place, it won't be a dead end—Because I am God, your personal God...I'd sell off the whole world to get you back, trade the creation just for you...That's how much I love you![9]

Attentive Listening

God often redeems the agony of loss through the words and actions of those who love us. While my family and friends often fumbled in their attempts to show sympathy, I was touched by their willingness to walk with me through the pain. Our adoption caseworker provided tremendous emotional support. Other helpful listeners in times of loss include fellow adoptive parents and mental health professionals who specialize in adoption, grief, or loss.

I particularly appreciated those who avoided doling out advice and simply made themselves available to listen. "Listening can be a greater service than speaking," writes Dietrich Bonhoeffer in *Life Together*:

> Just as love to God begins with listening to His Word, so the beginning of love for the brethren is learning to listen to them. It is God's love for us that He not only

gives us His Word but also lends us His ear. So it is His
work that we do for our brother when we learn to listen
to him.[10]

Bonhoeffer emphasizes that we must avoid the impatient "kind
of listening with half an ear that presumes already to know what the
other person has to say" or focuses on how we're going to respond.
Rather, we must practice attentive listening. "We should listen with
the ears of God that we may speak the Word of God,"[11] and reflect
hope to those who feel hopeless.

When I can't voice prayers, listening friends speak with God on
my behalf. Their presence assures me of God's presence. Their prayers
remind me God has not forgotten me.

God Is Enough

During my grieving process, I found hope as I read the letters
of my favorite biblical hero—the apostle Paul. In one of his letters to the Corinthians, Paul gives an account of his own suffering,
explaining that he had been thrown in prison frequently, flogged
severely five times, beaten with rods three times, stoned once, ship-
wrecked three times; that he had been in danger from rivers, bandits,
and from his own countrymen (just to name a few); and had been
hungry, thirsty, cold, and naked.

While my own losses pale in comparison to Paul's suffering, I
don't believe Paul's intent was to trump my heartache by proving
how much worse he had it than I do. Rather, it was his way of saying,
"Been there. Done that."

Paul hated suffering as much as the rest of us. He describes his
"thorn in the flesh," some kind of a chronic physical challenge he
begged the Lord to heal. God's response to him was, "My grace is
sufficient for you, for my power is made perfect in weakness"[12]

As I worked through my grief, I focused on the fact that God's
grace is indeed sufficient. He has engraved me on the palm of His
hands; He's not going to forget me or my heart's desire. He promises

to lavish comfort on me—to turn my weeping into laughter and to invade my grief with joy.[13] I'll never be disappointed when I rejoice in the hope I have in God.

■ ■ ■

As Robert and I endured the series of adoption losses, we sometimes felt like giving up. But like Joe and Peggy Bentz, we believed God would somehow redeem our crushed hopes. A week after our latest canceled adoption, Karen and Blaine, a six-months-pregnant couple, asked to meet us. When Blaine announced he was fairly certain he wanted to parent, I felt as if the air had been sucked from my lungs—again. But Robert and I continued to meet with them during the remainder of their pregnancy.

At four o'clock one morning, Blaine called and announced, "You have a baby boy. What do you want to name him?"

Four hours later, Blaine and Karen's pregnancy counselor called and told us, "Blaine really wants to parent this baby. Give him time to decide."

The following morning she called again. "Blaine and Karen have signed relinquishment papers. You will meet your son tomorrow."

On February 29, 1996, Robert, Ben, and I walked through the doors of our adoption agency to meet baby Joshua. The long wait was over. We had arrived as a family of three. Minutes later, we headed home—a family of four.

8

Out-of-Diaper Experience

Adopting a "Grown-up"

On a glorious Mother's Day, 30 members of the Christianson and Holmes clans gathered in our niece's backyard to celebrate her college graduation. Balancing a paper plate loaded with a hot dog and salad, I dragged a canvas lawn chair near where an aunt and uncle from the Holmes side of the family were sitting.

Although I hadn't seen Suzanne and Jamie Chandler in five years, our niece had kept us apprised of their plans to adopt. I plopped into my chair and without preamble, said, "I heard you're adopting two children from Russia. Tell me *everything.*"

Their eyes lit up. "We just returned from our first trip to Russia, where we met our children," said Suzanne. She reached under her chair. "We've got pictures!"

"Lots and lots of pictures," added Jamie, grinning.

Suzanne handed me five of her favorite photos. She pointed to images of a smiling six-year-old boy and a sweet-looking five-year-old girl. "This is Andy and Juliana," announced the proud mama.

"Are they biological siblings?"

The new parents shook their heads.

Then my husband, Robert, joined us. He, too, examined the photos and inquired, "Are they siblings?"

"They are now," responded Suzanne.

"What do you know about their backgrounds?" asked Robert.

"We have some information about their backgrounds and we see ourselves as guardians of their stories," responded Suzanne carefully. "When they're the right age, we'll give them their story and they can decide with whom to share it."

I smiled, delighted Suzanne and Jamie had come up with a respectful yet firm way to deflect questions they didn't feel comfortable answering.

I thumbed through the photos again and my heart skipped a beat as I mentally absorbed a photo of the proud parents—silly grins plastered on their faces—hugging their children for the first time. Vivid memories of the day Robert and I met our own children surfaced. I recalled our silly grins and breathed a silent prayer of thanks for the privilege of vicariously participating in Jamie and Suzanne's sacred moment—the moment when the world shrank and their family was created.

The Older, the Better

When Suzanne and Jamie chose to adopt "older" children—defined as children between the ages of 2 and 18—they confronted the prevalent societal notion that adopting infants and toddlers is preferable to adopting older children. "There's an expectation that younger kids are more desirable," says Suzanne. She and Jamie were offered opportunities to adopt much younger children, and passed. "I like older kids," declares Suzanne. "To me, *they* are more desirable."

Kim Felder agrees. In her job as a Wendy's Wonderful Kids recruiter for Los Angeles County, she gets to know the personalities and proclivities of the foster children with whom she works. "When parents adopt an older child, they can make more of a love match," she explains. They can look for a child with whom they share common ground, such as an introvert, an extrovert, a creative child, a sports-minded child, or an outdoorsy child.

Increasing numbers of people are choosing to adopt older children. Nearly 21,000 children per year—many of whom are classified as older children—are adopted internationally. And at least 50,000 children per year—children whose average age is seven—are adopted from U.S. foster care.[1]

While many people assume adopting an older child is riskier than adopting a newborn, that isn't necessarily the case. Amy and Jeff birthed their first son and adopted their son Nik from India when he was almost four. Because Nik had been institutionalized all his life, Amy and Jeff worried he'd have attachment issues and exhibit asocial behavior. "But it didn't happen," says Amy. "He attached himself to us very, very quickly."

Amy attributes Nik's rapid bonding partly to his orphanage caregivers, who thoroughly prepared him to meet his new family. Six weeks before the couple traveled to India, they sent Nik a photo album containing pictures of Jeff, Amy, his big brother, the house, and the cat. "Nik was excited to meet us," recalls Amy. "He shook our hands seriously and then spontaneously hugged Jeff."

Amy and Jeff's fears regarding Nik's sociability were unfounded. "Nik is the most social child I've ever met," says Amy, laughing. "He walks into a room and works it, going around and shaking hands with people."

At summer camp, five-year-old Nik instantly pinpointed the person in charge, introduced himself, and began making himself useful to that person. "He does that at school and in Sunday school, as well," says Amy. While she and Jeff are alert to potential attachment problems, they haven't noticed any. They attribute Nik's gregarious nature to "a survival skill he learned at the orphanage."

Amy and Jeff were pleasantly surprised by Nik's independence. "That first night in the hotel, we laid Nik's pajamas out. He put them on, walked into the bathroom, brushed his teeth, crawled into bed, and slept through the entire night. Jeff and I looked at each other and said, 'This is brilliant! Why didn't we do this with our older son?'"

While Amy wishes she'd been able to hold Nik when he was an infant and mourns not having any baby pictures of him, she and

Jeff are thrilled they adopted an older child. "You know so much more about your child in terms of health risks and mental development," she reflects. And older children are much more independent than infants—they can bathe themselves, play with their parents and siblings, and even help with chores. "If we were to adopt again, we would definitely adopt a child who's at least two," says Amy.

A Family Affair

Expanding your family through adoption is a family affair. If you have other children, it's vital that you take their feelings into account when deciding whether to adopt an older child.

During the time Karen Kingsbury and her husband Don contemplated adopting three boys from Haiti, they consulted with their three birth children, then ages ten, seven, and two. "We asked them, 'What do you think? You're sharing Mommy and Daddy forever. You're sharing your home and your heritage and your inheritance—everything about your life. When you get married, these boys will be at your wedding. They're going to be your family long after we're gone.'"

Karen cautions prospective parents: "No matter how passionate you are about adopting, if your kids are not 100 percent as passionate, it is not going to work; it's going to be heartbreak." She believes the "preventative discussions" she and Don had with their children helped them "own" the adoption and erased resentment issues that might have surfaced had they not prepared their children adequately.

The addition of a new child to the family knocks everyone off balance. In *Our Own: Adopting and Parenting the Older Child,* Trish Maskew explains that your other children may feel threatened the new arrival will change their place in the family. They fear you'll love them less, or that you won't need or want them once the new sibling arrives.[2] While they're excited about their new brother or sister, they're uneasy about sharing you with a stranger, and about explaining the new sibling to their friends.

Parents can get so wrapped up in helping their newest child feel comfortable and accepted that they ignore the adjustment crisis their other kids are undergoing. Maskew's advice: "Set aside fifteen to twenty minutes each day to talk with each of your children one-on-one about their feelings toward the new arrival."[3]

What's in a Name?

Your child may wish to choose a new name to celebrate joining your family. When Jesse and Carole were fostering a six-year-old in hopes of adopting him, they and their son decided to change his first name. Eager to participate in choosing his new moniker, their son suggested his favorite names: Pikachu, Squirtle, and Charizard. Not wishing to saddle their son with the name of his favorite Pokémon character, Jesse and Carole quickly redirected him, steering him toward three more appropriate names. Their son eventually decided "Isaiah" was a good fit.

Parents who adopt internationally often Americanize their child's name or meld some portion of their child's original name into the new American name. Jeanne Marie Laskas, author of *Growing Girls,* writes that she and her husband couldn't figure out how to do this with their daughters, Anna and Sasha:

> Anna's Chinese name is Gu Yu Qian. We tried Anna Gu Levy or Anne Gu Yu Levy and everything sounded ridiculous and apologetic. "Levy" is so Jewish; you throw Chinese into it and the whole thing sounds too eager to please. So with both girls we decided they'd head into life with two names; they'd have their American names and they'd grow up knowing their Chinese names, too.[4]

If you're considering changing your child's name, carefully assess your motives. Some parents change their child's name simply because they don't like it. Some do so to protect their child from a dangerous birth parent. Many parents believe changing their child's name helps both parent and child claim one another on a deeper level.

Sandra Fortier, a social worker with experience in foster care and adoption, cautions that changing your child's name may damage your child's already fragile self-esteem. In *Fostering Families TODAY* magazine, she writes.

> Our first name is inextricably linked to our identity and self-esteem…If parents change the name because they don't like it, the child may consciously or unconsciously view that as a rejection of his or her pre-adoption identity or even as a rejection of his or her "true" identity. In short, if you reject your child's first name, your child may perceive this as rejecting him or her as a person.[5]

Fortier suggests changing your child's middle name, since most children don't have a significant connection to their middle name. Doing so helps you "claim the child and feel more connected without significant potential for harming the child's sense of identity."[6]

Suzanne and Jamie Chandler gave their children new first names and kept their Russian names as middle names. "People frowned on us for giving them new first names, telling us we were changing their identity," explains Suzanne. "But really, when you adopt children, aren't you doing that anyway? We're changing our children's identity from *orphanage child* to *family child;* from *one who lives by rules and structure* to *one who learns to make good independent choices.*"

Suzanne, a teacher in a school district with a significant Russian immigrant population, worries that people in her community make prejudicial assumptions about children with "immigrant-sounding names." When school staff members hear a Russian name, they assume the family speaks Russian at home. Those children are routed into underfunded English-as-a-Second-Language tracks and steered toward vocational, rather than academic classes. "I don't want my kids carrying names into the school district that might trigger subtle prejudice," Suzanne vows.

She and Jamie call their children by both their American and

Russian names, and note that if Andy and Juliana prefer to be called by their Russian names, they'll honor the request.

Whether you change your child's first name, middle name, or opt not to change it at all, remember that your child is first and foremost God's child. As you nurture your child to love the Lord, he will grow into his name and will do it proud.

The Language of Love

One of the biggest advantages of adopting older children is their ability to communicate. During the months children adopted internationally are acquiring their new language, you can communicate through hand motions, body language, laughter, and song. Karen Kingsbury's sons spoke only Haitian Creole when they first arrived.

Karen yearned to ask her boys, "How are you doing? Do you miss Haiti? What are you excited about?" Instead, Karen, Don, and their three birth children spent three months pointing at people and objects and repeating, "Cup. Mommy. Grandma."

But the family had one common language: praise music. In the Haitian orphanage, the boys had learned praise songs in English. Before bedtime, Don strummed his guitar while the entire family worshiped joyfully together through song. "Singing became our foundational communication tool," explains Karen.

Unlike internationally-adopted children who are acquiring language skills, older children adopted domestically can describe their feelings. "Many of these children have been abused and neglected and have spent part of their lives in an environment that retarded their growth," says Kim Felder. "Like plants in dry soil, they hang on, but they don't thrive."

But given fertile soil, appropriate stimulus, and a little "miracle grow," older children bloom like a flowering plant that has been pruned, nurtured, and watered. Once they settle in and feel safe in a loving, stable environment, they begin chatting, says Kim, the

Names and Promises

■ ■ ■

In the Old Testament, God sometimes changes people's names in conjunction with a life-changing promise He makes. When God promises Abram he will be the father of many nations, God changes his name to *Abraham* (meaning "the father of numerous offspring"). When God blesses Abraham's wife to become the mother of nations, He changes her name from Sarai (meaning "bitter; contentious one") to *Sarah* (meaning "princess").[7]

Later, Abraham's grandson, Jacob (meaning, "the heel-holder; the supplanter"), gets his name changed to Israel (meaning "he who prevails with God") when God reiterates the promise He made to Abraham.[8]

In the New Testament, Jesus changes His disciple Simon's name to Peter to highlight Peter's new identity as His adopted son.[9] Peter, whose name means "rock," becomes a builder and spiritual leader of the early Christian church.

Finally, all who begin a new life united with the Messiah are promised a new name. Our new name indicates a close association with God; it's a reminder our heavenly Father adopted us.[10]

mother of eight (six of whom were adopted). "It's wonderful, because I can look at my kids and say, 'You look upset. Why?'"

Older children use words to indicate the foods they like and dislike, the clothes they prefer to wear, and the way they want to decorate their bedroom. Together, you can discuss their cultural traditions, their birth family, and their favorite activities.

Older children also have words (often ones you won't approve of) to express their anger and frustration. When Aimeé and Tommy Poché traveled to Peru to adopt their 22-month-old daughter, they learned she had four additional siblings. Eighteen months later, they adopted her siblings, ages 15, 13, 9, and 21 months.

The transition was hardest on the 15-year-old, who had played a "mother" role to her younger siblings in the orphanage. "She had never been in a family and she had the misguided expectation that 'family' meant 'fun,'" says Aimeé. Uprooted from everything familiar and placed in a strange culture, city, and family, their daughter alternately demanded to go back to Peru and agonized over why she felt so angry when she finally had the home she'd always yearned for.

In addition to the challenges they face with their 15-year-old, Aimeé and Tommy's 5-year-old child rarely speaks and is two years below the norm in motor skills and toilet training. Two of their other children are three grades behind their peers academically.

While Aimeé and Tommy had no idea how emotionally draining it would be to parent the five siblings, they view their children as their mission field. Their mission is to provide their children with hope and a future. "When you're called to adopt an older child, God has already paved the way for you," says Aimeé. Besides, she reflects, "We live one time on this earth. I say, 'Live hard.'"

Heavy Baggage

While an older child may arrive in your home with only a garbage bag of possessions, she hauls heavy emotional baggage. One mom, who began fostering her daughter when the girl was four (and later adopted her), says, "She remembers her birth family, so we talk openly with her about them and allow her to vent her feelings about them."

At first, the adoptive mom felt reluctant to encourage discussions about her daughter's birth parents. "I wanted to be 'Mom' and the only mom. It took me a while to accept that my daughter remembers several moms: her biological mom and four other foster moms."

The fact that an older child comes with a history can be both an advantage and a disadvantage. On one hand, you will usually receive information about your child's medical history, past placements, and developmental milestones. You'll be able to help her process memories about her birth family, her foster family, or her orphanage. If your child experienced prenatal drug exposure, she can participate in developmental testing that will indicate how that exposure will likely affect her.

On the other hand, an emotionally scarred child usually feels rejected, unloved, and abandoned. She may lack basic skills such as how to use the toilet and how to eat with utensils. She may be afraid to leave the house or attend school. She may have received poor education and spiritual training. A child adopted as a teenager is likely not ready for independence; she probably doesn't know how to cook, plan a budget, keep a job, or pay bills.

A child who has been disappointed by adults and uprooted for most of her life is unlikely to trust adults. She may cope by clinging to you every waking moment; she may withdraw or act politely reserved; or she may rage, bully, manipulate, and act resentful about everything you say and do. While she may love you, she may not be able to express affection or to accept your love.

But isn't love enough? Isn't love—and the promise of a permanent home—enough to conquer a child's pre-existing history of neglect, abuse, and instability? The answer, in a word, is *no*. Love alone is not enough. Love is the piece every parent starts with and builds upon.

Unpacking the Baggage

One mom compares adopting an older child to getting married: "You both bring things from your past and you have to commit to like each other." But learning to love and trust a new family can be a slow, arduous process for an older child. If you expect your child to express gratitude and joy because you adopted him, you may be in for a shock. Most older children struggle with deep-seated feelings of loss and are reluctant to believe they'll remain a permanent fixture in your family.

You must learn to accept your child's lack of gratitude with grace. You must be willing to love unconditionally—from the moment your child enters your life—without expecting love in return. Your patient presence provides the backbone of consistent support that will help your child unravel years of instability. As you and your child share experiences and become familiar with one another, you'll mutually develop a sense of trust and allegiance.

"Adopting an older child is not for the faint of heart, but your child is worth the fight," says one mom who adopted her daughter from foster care. You must have a well-developed sense of humor and superb problem-solving skills. In addition, you must possess three critical qualities: inner strength, flexibility, and a willingness to seek support.

Inner strength. Parenting a child adopted at an older age requires enormous stamina. It's imperative that married couples head into adoption with a strong marriage and that single parents tap into a tremendous support system. "Don't bring a challenge into an already challenged situation," recommends Reuben, a dad who fostered an eight-year-old. "If you're not capable and resolved and bolstered to face challenges, you'll wear down in a hurry."

Flexibility. You must be long-sighted, not short-sighted. Enthusiastically celebrate your child's small successes as you guide him toward dependence by providing him with a stable home, medical care, and educational opportunities. Then guide him toward independence by equipping him with the skills and savvy he needs to live on his own. When you consider that 60 percent of the children who age out of foster care end up in prison or in the homeless population, your loving intervention bestows a life-changing gift to a child who might otherwise have been forced to fend for himself at age 18.

Interestingly, children adopted as teenagers aren't always anxious to live on their own when they come of age. Because they've missed out on so many of the basic childhood staples, such as birthday parties, holiday celebrations, and riding bikes, they often prefer to "nest." "Kids who have survived horrific early years typically need their parents several years longer than other children," writes Rita Laws in *Fostering Families TODAY.* "Maturity seems to take a little longer, but it comes."[11]

Your child will be an adult in your life a whole lot longer than he'll be a child. The relational seeds you plant in your child now may result in a healthy adult relationship between you and your child. Never underestimate the value of instilling a sense of *family.*

Willingness to seek support. Suzanne and Jamie Chandler expected their children to regress in all areas of development once Andy and Juliana joined their family. They expected bed-wetting. They expected sadness and anger from their children. Before they brought their children home from Russia, Jamie and Suzanne scheduled full medical, psychological, and developmental assessments with an adoption medicine specialist.

In anticipation of the issues that were bound to arise once their children became acclimated to their new home, Suzanne and Jamie planned monthly visits to a family therapist. When issues began to surface, the entire family was comfortably established in a routine therapy environment.

Prior to adopting their children, Suzanne lurked on an Internet discussion list for adoptive parents and read adoption blogs. "I noticed typical concerns parents had and I researched them." Rather than desperately scrabbling for information while embroiled in crisis,

Suzanne anticipated stressors and planned how to deal with them while she still had energy and emotional reserves.

Never hesitate to ask for help. That's the motto of all parents who adopt older children. Tone your parenting muscles by enrolling in child development and parenting courses at local community colleges, hospitals, social service agencies, or adoption organizations.

If you're adopting a foster child, push for adoption support. While you can't change what happened in your child's past, you *can* change what happens in his future. Your parental responsibility is to obtain the help your child needs. *Before* you finalize your adoption, learn whether your child is eligible for federal- or state-funded adoption assistance or both. These programs provide services such as counseling, medical and dental care, therapeutic day care, parent training, and they subsidize specialized educational programs.

In addition to seeking support services for your child, obtain support for yourself. "Have somebody you can call and talk to during the hard days," recommends one mom. Join an adoptive parent support group and connect with families who have adopted older children. And don't neglect to build in "me" time.

In *Hot Flashes, Warm Bottles,* Nancy London writes, "When kids are given a clear message that mom loves them a lot, but has a life of her own, they are highly adaptable." She recommends sitting down with your family to agree on specific down times for yourself. "Instead of a child thinking she must have done something wrong for mommy to go away behind a closed door, he or she can begin seeing this as normal, predictable behavior."[12]

The World's Longest Play Date

During your child's transition from out-of-home placement (foster care) or an orphanage to your home, you'll probably wonder whether you and your child are ever going to attach to one another. You and your child may feel like participants in the world's longest play date, hovering around one another uncertainly, tentatively reaching out toward one another and inexplicably pulling back; reveling in a budding friendship one minute and shedding tears of frustration the next.

This behavior is normal and usually lasts from a few months to a couple of years. It helps to remind yourself that your child has been uprooted from everything familiar. No matter how dismal his former living conditions might have been, he grieves the loss of a family culture he understands. He probably doesn't know how to express his grief; he's more concerned with surviving in a new family culture.

You can increase your child's comfort level by providing him with consistency, rest, and time to get used to his new surroundings. Suzanne Chandler calls it *cocooning*. "The normal activities of everyday life overstimulate my kids the way other kids get revved up at Christmastime," she says. During those initial months in your home, try to think of your child as a "newborn" to your family. She'll need time and space to observe and absorb your family culture.

Suzanne and Jamie gave their children plenty of "down time" at first, limiting their interaction to relatives and close friends who were regular fixtures in their everyday lives. Suzanne obtained the orphanage's schedule and adhered to it so her children didn't have to wonder, "What am I supposed to do next?" On the days she and Jamie exposed their children to something new, such as a trip to Costco, they made sure to follow a predictable routine during the next few days.

Parents who adopt children from foster care agree: Consistent parenting is the key to helping a child adjust. "If your child napped at her foster home, keep her naptime consistent," recommends one mom.

And while it sounds counterintuitive, it's also important to assign your child some chores so she can settle into a routine. The sooner you begin treating her like one of the family and not like a houseguest, the sooner she'll begin to feel like she belongs.

"When your son screams at you in anger, don't threaten to send him back to foster care," advises another mom. A child who has lived in multiple out-of-home placements often acts out to test how awful his behavior has to be in order to get sent back to foster care. It's your job to teach him people don't go away. Hone your sense of empathy and acknowledge that your life will be child-focused for a very, very long time.

When you experience nail-biting moments that cause you to holler, "Heaven help me!" be assured help is only a prayer away. God is the perfect rescuer, writes Grace Fox in *10-Minute Time-Outs for Moms*. He's stronger, wiser, kinder, and smarter than we are, and He's waiting to rush to our rescue. He knows why our children act and react the way they do. "He knows their strengths and weaknesses and what He must do to conform them to Jesus Christ's image."[13]

When we're weary, writes Fox, God reminds us strength comes from Him—the one who created heaven and earth and holds the universe in place, the one who never slumbers nor sleeps. As we wait on God, He strengthens us, equips us, and enables us to perform our parenting tasks with excellence.

International Intrigue

Planes, Trains, and Orphanages

I walked into the orphanage and glanced around to get my bearings. White metal cribs, lined up end to end, packed every available space in the room. Twenty cribs. Twenty babies. Taking shallow breaths to filter the overpowering stench of urine that permeated the warm, humid air, I approached the first crib. Its occupant, a baby who looked to be about six months old, lay sprawled on his back, crying. His only clothing was a thin cotton cloth tied loosely around his bottom. He raised pencil-thin arms in a plea for me to hold him. I bent and carefully lifted the fragile baby from his crib. In one quick, instinctive motion, he wrapped his spindly arms around my neck, tucked his head into the crook of my shoulder, and stopped crying.

Minutes later, sensing he was safe, the little guy loosened his grip and peeked at me. Noticing my gold watch band and wedding ring, he tentatively rubbed his fingers over their shiny surface. The brown-eyed cutie gradually became more and more animated; he babbled, pointed at the other babies, and played pat-a-cake. As I watched him transform, I invented a happy ending: he'd go home to a family who nourished him with plenty of food and love.

But this little boy, who was 18 months old—not 6 months old, as I had estimated—had no such happy ending in store. Abandoned by his parents because they had no money to feed another mouth, the malnourished baby was waiting to die. At the end of the day, I settled him back in his crib and slowly turned away, feeling as if my heart had been hacked into pieces.

Made in China

During that trip to Haiti I came face-to-face with the poverty and hopelessness in which many of the world's children live. Some of the children I met were waiting to be adopted by families from throughout the world. Those fortunate few would be given a priceless gift: the opportunity to grow to adulthood—their bodies, minds, and spirits nourished to overflowing.

The number of children from other countries adopted by U.S. families has more than doubled during the past ten years, to nearly 21,000. About 80 percent of the children adopted internationally come from China, Guatemala, Russia, and South Korea.[1] Why do American families choose to travel to other continents to adopt when more than 120,000 children in U.S. foster care wait to be adopted?[2]

There are many reasons, such as...

- You have family ties or heart-ties to a particular country.

- You sense a calling or a vocation to adopt internationally.

- You can predict the time frame for intercountry adoption more accurately than for domestic adoption.

- You're highly likely to adopt the child with whom you are matched.

- You're aware of all adoption fees you'll pay before you begin the process.

- You don't have to self-market (unlike those who seek to adopt a healthy U.S. infant).

- You can often adopt healthy infants (of at least three months old) or toddlers.

- Many countries welcome over-40 parents.
- Many countries welcome parents who already have birth or adopted children.
- Many countries welcome single parents.

Another reason parents opt for intercountry adoption is because the U.S. public adoption system turns them off. Many elect to gamble on the unknown entity of a foreign government, claiming our overburdened, underfunded system feels untrustworthy and fails to provide a timely, effective means for transitioning children from foster care into adoptive homes.

Nearly everyone who adopts internationally does so for humanitarian reasons, recognizing that the severe poverty suffered by so many children born in developing countries all but eliminates their chances of living a long, healthy life. And while orphanage life does constitute a "community" of sorts, it's nothing like being a cherished member of a family.

Exclusively Yours

One of the most prevalent reasons people choose intercountry adoption is to avoid the possibility of contact with birth parents. Many adoptive parents want their claim on their child to be exclusive. When parents receive their referral or are "matched" with a child, they become emotionally attached to that child. They want to bypass any possibility a birth parent will challenge the adoption or will show up at some point, demanding to be part of his or her child's life.

But life does not begin at adoption, writes Trish Maskew in *Our Own: Adopting and Parenting the Older Child.* "Our children have a history before us and it does not include us."[3] She believes that discounting the existence of a child's birth family discounts the child.

It's becoming more common, even for children who were abandoned, to identify and establish contact with their birth parents later in life. "An abandoned child still has birth parents," explains Sunday Silver, Director of U.S. Programs for Holt International Children's Services in Eugene, Oregon. "It's important to acknowledge that, respect it, and allow your child to talk about his or her birth parents."

When Eileen and Brad's son, Marcus (now 21), was 14, the family took a trip to the ocean. Each of them wrote a note, put it in a bottle, and threw their bottle into the mouth of the river that flows into the ocean. As Marcus tossed his bottle, he remarked, "Maybe my birth mother will find it."

"It was a sweet moment," says Eileen, "and a natural opportunity to remind him his birth mother was surely thinking of him, too."

Eileen and Brad have often discussed visiting Korea with Marcus, but he adamantly refuses to go. "As Marcus grew older, he truly developed the identity of 'Asian American' rather than 'Korean adoptee,'" says Brad.

Reluctant to push the issue, his parents told Marcus that if he ever decides he wants to visit Korea—whether it's a family vacation, a private trip, a structured "homeland tour," or an attempt to contact his foster family and/or his birth mother—they'll pay for his trip.

Some adopted children yearn for an opportunity to meet their birth parents. Ryan and Amanda Robbins' eight-year-old daughter, Meera, sometimes asks, "Can we find my birth family in India? Can we go see them?"

Ryan and Amanda, who have very little information about Meera's birth mother, answer honestly, "I'm afraid not. Calcutta is a big city and we don't know where she is." The Robbinses are traveling to India this year—not to search for Meera's birth family, but to re-introduce Meera to her birth culture. "When we're in India, Meera won't be the minority for once; Amanda and I will be the ones who look different from everyone else," says Ryan.

Rather than feeling fearful of your child's birth family or trying to erase them from your child's memory, it's important to acknowledge that your child can simultaneously love you and have intense

feelings about his original family. In *Beyond Good Intentions*, Cheri
Register writes,

> This curiosity, even when it evolves into longing and then
> into searching, doesn't negate the value of your parent-
> hood or diminish your importance in your child's life. It's
> not rejection, not disloyalty. It is not even about you…if
> you love your child and truly want what's best for him,
> you will cheer him on in his quest for a familial and cul-
> tural history. And he will love you back. If you set yourself
> up in competition with your child's other parents, you
> will likely lose.[4]

A Shot in the Arm

Intercountry adoption carries an aura of romanticism. Relatives,
friends, and even strangers will clamor to coo over your imported
doll, admiring her as if she's a porcelain specimen in a museum display: "Ooh, what a cutie! Where'd you get her? She's so tiny!" And
then comes the kicker, asked even to parents of infants: "Does she
speak English?"

You sheepishly absorb the gushing goodwill, tucking it away in
your emotional bank account. From time to time, you may need to
make withdrawals from the goodwill bank; not everyone welcomes
a child adopted from another country. Friends wonder: "Why'd you
go all the way to another country to adopt when so many children
in the U.S. are waiting to be adopted?"

It's a legitimate question, especially considering that intercountry
adoption presents many of the same risk factors as adopting from
U.S. foster care. The birth parents of a child adopted internationally have experienced extreme poverty, physical or mental illness,
alcohol or drug abuse, political or cultural stigmas, or other issues
that make parenting impossible.

You'll receive little reliable medical information about your
child. You should not trust medical records, assessments, or treatments completed in developing countries; even routine vaccines

given to your child may have been outdated or not properly refrigerated.

"A child's medical condition might be understated in hope that a child might be more readily adopted," writes Lois Ruskai Melina in *Raising Adopted Children*. On the other hand, medical conditions are sometimes overstated "to enable a child to meet governmental regulations that require a child to have a 'special need' to be adopted internationally."[5]

You should assume your child will have had poor prenatal care and will more than likely be malnourished and at least slightly developmentally delayed. She may suffer from intestinal parasites, anemia, or rickets. While some internationally adopted children are fortunate to live in foster homes where they receive loving, one-on-one care, most live in crowded orphanages with caretakers who are overworked, indifferent, or even abusive. Your child will be at risk for needing long-term medical or psychological care or both.

After you receive your referral, you should have your child's medical records examined by a pediatrician who specializes in adoption medicine. Adoption medicine specialists work with families through the entire process, from referral to travel to transitioning and beyond. During a pre-adoption consultation, your specialist will review your child's available medical records, pictures, and videos. Typically, your specialist will evaluate your child's developmental milestones, growth patterns, and size (particularly her head size, which can indicate malnutrition, fetal alcohol exposure, or certain birth defects).

If a videotape of your child is available, it will help the pediatrician assess hearing disorders, language development, and social development. Based on your pediatrician's knowledge of the medical issues routinely associated with institutionalized children from a particular country, your specialist can predict your child's future medical or developmental needs and can provide insights as to how your child may attach to you.

Many adoption medicine specialists offer an invaluable service to parents: they're on-call to consult with you during the time you travel to meet your child. Pediatricians from The Center for Adoption Medicine in Seattle provide pre-travel prescriptions for antibiotics; eye ointment; medication for skin infections; scabies treatment; multivitamins with iron, and sterile needles and syringes. Then, during adoption travel, the pediatricians are available via e-mail or phone to advise you if you're faced with surprise medical or developmental concerns or illness.

Once your child arrives home, your adoption medicine specialist will refer you to adoption-savvy pediatricians in your area or will conduct your child's post-placement medical evaluation. Deborah Borchers, a founding member of the American Academy of Pediatrics Section on Adoption and Foster Care, recommends that the post-placement consultation include "a review of all medical records, a complete physical examination, and diagnostic testing, all taking into consideration the child's past."[6]

You can help your child's pediatrician by learning as much as possible about your child's history. If you have the opportunity to visit your child's orphanage or foster home before bringing her to your home, observe the way in which your child's caregivers interact with her. Ask the caregivers about your child's likes and dislikes, about her personality, and about the amount and type of social contact she has with other children and adults.

Extravagant Love

If you're feeling uncertain about whether you're equipped to meet the needs of a child from another country, you'll find direction in Paul's first letter to the Corinthians. In chapters 12 and 13, Paul explains that God gives each of us something practical to do that helps heal the wounds of our broken, imperfect world. For those who feel drawn toward loving the world's children, that "something" may be adoption. As Frederick Buechner puts it, God's call on your life "is the one in which your deep gladness and the world's deep need meet—something that not only makes you happy but that the world needs to have done."[7]

As you love your child with everything you've got, you'll sense a growing assurance that you are, indeed, participating with God in a miracle. Scott Church and Audrey Laxton, who adopted their daughter Claire LanDu from China, view every day with her as a miracle. Their love affair with Claire began when they received a fuzzy snapshot of a round-faced 12-month-old whose vacant expression revealed nothing about the little soul who hid inside. Their love intensified in the hallway of a Chengdu hotel, where Scott and Audrey first met Claire.

Scott recalls, "She was looking right at me. The halls resonated with the crying of confused babies who didn't understand the sudden chaos or the strange new arms that were taking them from familiar ones. But *this* little girl was peaceful—even serene. As I approached, her gaze never left me. When I reached for her, she came willingly into my arms. Fear vanished and a wave of joy washed over me. I wept, my body quaking." The first picture Audrey took captures Claire looking up in peaceful trust at her tearful daddy, both of them surprised by joy.

Four years have passed since the day Scott and Audrey met Claire, but their love affair with their daughter continues fiercer than ever. "We have been called to walk beside her—to expose her to things that will enrich her," says Scott. "We have been called to do our best to model values we hope she will make her own. We have been called to pray daily for God's loving hand on her life, and for the grace and wisdom we need, as parents."[8]

As they continue to discover their daughter, Scott and Audrey inhale the healing peace that comes from enjoying the simplest moments of daily life: snuggling with Claire in an easy chair, watching Disney princess videos, holding hands, and walking along the beach. Their family is, indeed, living a miracle.

God's Ongoing Help

■ ■ ■

God doesn't just give you the desire to adopt a child and then bow out, abandoning you to muddle through on your own. God gives you abilities and invites you to partner *with* Him as you use those gifts:

- *He gives the gift of knowledge.* That means developing an awareness of and compassion for children who need a family.

- *He gives the gift of faith.* That means trusting God to help you find the child who needs you—the child you need.

- *He gives the gift of wisdom.* That means patiently negotiating with a government official who threatens to derail your adoption.

- *He gives the gift of healing.* That means committing to support and nurture your child, especially during the moments when you secretly wonder whether you've made the right decision in adopting her.

And God equips you with a special gift that's the best one of all: the ability to love extravagantly. "Love cares more for others than for self," writes the apostle Paul. "Love puts up with anything. Love always looks for the best, never looks back, but keeps going to the end."[9]

10

Culture Club

Extreme Makeover: Adoption Edition

During my trip to Haiti, I gained a sense of the disorientation a young child must feel when he's plucked from familiar sights, sounds, and smells and permanently transplanted into an adoptive family. In Haiti, mine was the only white face among a sea of black ones. Children and adults alike pointed at me and called, "Blan, blan!" *("White, white!").* The cadence of the Haitian Creole language, while beautiful, was indecipherable at first. My roiling stomach, which longed for milk and fruit, reluctantly acclimated to a diet of rice and beans.

Knowing my host family was curiously watching my every move, I attempted to fit into their routine, terrified I'd make a mistake. Even with 40 years of life experience behind me, I felt alternately exhilarated and exhausted as I absorbed the unfamiliar culture. I can only imagine the fearful wonder that envelops an adopted child during the transition to his or her new family.

Ch-Ch-Changes

"Information overload" doesn't begin to describe the way your long-awaited child feels when she arrives in your family. She's simultaneously giddy, bewildered, and terrified. It doesn't matter whether she's 6 months old, 6 years old, or 16 years old; she instinctively senses her world has been turned inside out. She may absorb her new surroundings with wide-eyed wonder, happily settling into your family as if she's always been there. Or she may transform into a hellion: howling, biting, scratching, and spitting. Sometimes she'll defiantly tilt her chin up, avoid eye contact, and act as if you don't exist. Other times, she may cling to you so long and so hard that you feel as if you've got a tree hugger permanently attached to the lower part of your body.

As you enthusiastically settle your child into her very own bedroom—one you've painstakingly decorated—she'll stare at you, glassy-eyed. She's used to sleeping in a room with 20 other children. You can expect your new child to be alternately enraptured and baffled over other "firsts": flushing a toilet, owning an endless supply of toys and clothes, attending church, eating the foods to which you're accustomed, and getting up-close-and-personal with a family pet. In fact, the very pet you consider "one of the family"

Seeing Jesus in the Light Switch

■ ■ ■

Upon arriving in your home, your child will experience a mind-boggling array of "firsts." When my friend Christy adopted her Haitian-born daughters, 4-year-old Mimi and 2-year-old Violet had never ridden in a car (not to mention an airplane), nor had they visited a grocery store. "They were fascinated by running water and by anything electrical, like the refrigerator, dishwasher, and microwave," says Christy. "When Mimi first turned on a light switch, she was convinced Jesus was in the light switch because in her mind, that was the only way the lights could possibly turn on."

Karen Kingsbury's three sons (also adopted from Haiti) were similarly entranced by electronics. "They were enthralled by the vacuum, particularly by the 'innards that made it go.' They regularly asked, 'Please, Mommy, can I use the machine?'"

may represent the source of protein your new child is accustomed to eating.

Immediately after your child arrives in your home, you can expect her to experience challenges such as difficulty falling asleep, fear of sleeping alone, or night terrors. She may have a variety of toileting problems: anxiety-induced diarrhea; constipation caused by dehydration and the sudden change in diet; bed-wetting; pants-wetting; and very likely, puzzlement about how—and when—to use a Western-style toilet.

Adjusting to a new diet is a major challenge for most children. While some children are offended by the strange smell and texture of our foods and eat very little, others gorge themselves.

When Karen Kingsbury's three sons lived on the streets of Port-au-Prince, Haiti, they survived by eating "dirt cakes," a mixture of dirt, clay, and water the local women baked in crumbly pottery. While they were in orphanage care, Karen estimates they ate about 800 calories a day of rice and beans. When they arrived in Karen and Don's home, the boys were shocked by the amount of food available to them.

Since the boys (then ages five and six) loved rice, Karen bought a rice maker, intending to allow them all the rice they could shovel into their mouths. Karen cooked them enough rice to feed a family of five. The boys devoured it in minutes. She cooked more rice. That disappeared instantly, too. So she cooked even more rice. "*Each* boy ate enough rice to feed a family of five," says Karen, laughing. "I thought, 'Where are they putting this stuff?'"

Children who have never had a full stomach are likely to eat voraciously during their first months home, fearing this sudden superabundance of food must be an anomaly. Some parents report they've observed their child trolling for scraps from the countertops or floor and hoarding food under beds, beneath couch cushions, and in dresser drawers. As your child digests the fact that plenty of food will always be available, the amount he eats—and the speed at which he gobbles it—will gradually level out.

The language barrier is an obstacle for families whose children are old enough to talk. After Christy adopted Mimi and Violet from Haiti, mother and daughters learned each other's language together. "My 4-year-old made it clear that as long as she was learning my language, I should learn hers as well." As Christy taught Mimi and Violet the English word for *cup,* they taught her the corresponding Creole word. "Both my girls laughed and laughed as I struggled to learn *banana* and *apple* in Creole."

While it's helpful to learn words and phrases in your child's language, a rudimentary knowledge of one another's language does little to alleviate the frustration of being unable to communicate thoughts and feelings. During the months your child is learning English, try to find an interpreter who will assist your family. You can locate interpreters through adoptive parent groups, churches, public libraries, nonprofit organizations, interpreter associations, and schools. Often, high school and college students who are studying a foreign language volunteer to interpret in order to fulfill a community service or internship requirement.

During the three months Mimi and Violet were mastering English, Mimi interpreted for 2-year-old Violet. "It was empowering for Mimi to be the interpreter," says Christy. "She felt very important—and she was."

Christy used the services of an interpreter when she took her daughters to the doctor about two weeks after they arrived in the U.S. "I thought the girls would be so happy to hear their language and I was anxious to have the interpreter translate a few things," she recalls. "The girls heard the interpreter say *hello* in Creole and started screaming. They continued screaming throughout the entire doctor visit. Thoughts of translation went right out the window."

Christy hoped her daughters would retain their Creole, but it vanished after about five months. "We have a tape of the girls speaking and singing in Creole. They love to listen to it and find it utterly astonishing that they once spoke a language they now no longer understand," says Christy.

When children become fluent in English, they often refuse to speak their first language and most of them eventually lose all recollection of that language. "Forgetting" a first language signals a child's decision to embrace all things American—most especially, her new family. Christy felt wistful when her daughters lost this critical component of their heritage. "I was determined to help the girls retain Creole," she says. "I had high hopes of dining with Haitian students, attending Haitian church services, and finding all sorts of ways to hear Creole."

But the reality of the commitment and the difficulty of helping her daughters retain Creole in an English-speaking culture quickly set in. Christy continues to offer her daughters opportunities to revisit their first language, allowing them to decide when they're ready to take advantage of those opportunities. "I'm hopeful they will find a time in their life to regain and feel competent with their language," she says.

Spicing Things Up

When you travel to another country to adopt, your family tree sprouts multicultural branches for all future generations. Your child's ethnic and cultural heritage becomes intertwined with your own. You'll discover, to your delight, that celebrating your child's heritage will expand your circle of friends and broaden your worldview.

Anne Baldwin, who was adopted domestically, is part Thai and East Indian. She has always been fascinated with Thailand. "Growing up, I read about it and tried to teach myself the language." She and her parents traveled to Thailand several times so they could experience the culture firsthand.

Anne, who's preparing to adopt a baby from Guatemala, believes parents shouldn't force "culture" on their child, but should routinely build cultural exploration into everyday life. She plans to introduce her child to Guatemalan culture by cooking Guatemalan foods, reading books, looking at pictures, and learning about Guatemala's history.

Brad and Eileen, who adopted their son, Marcus, from Korea 21 years ago, have melded their natural interests—politics, reading, and cooking—with an ongoing immersion into Marcus's birth culture. "I keep an eye on Korean politics, read Korean literature and Korean history, and subscribe to *KoreAm Journal*, a magazine published by the Korean American community," says Brad.

As Marcus grew, his family attended Korean Lunar New Year celebrations, enrolled in Korean language classes, ate at Korean restaurants, and shopped at Korean grocery stores. Eileen, who loves to cook, learned to make traditional Korean dishes. "All the way through his late teens, Marcus requested his mom's Korean meals for his birthday dinner," says Brad.

Jamie Dailey, who adopted her daughter from China, makes a concerted effort to help her three-year-old retain as much Chinese culture as possible. "Our daughter enjoys having her 'China' books read to her; she'll choose those books over any others. She's thrilled with videos about China and the Chinese language." Some of her daughter's favorites include *Big Bird in China; Follow Jade; Muzzy Mandarin;* and a DVD of a song festival from her home province of Guangxi.

The Daileys celebrate two Chinese holidays with friends and extended family: Chinese New Year and the Autumn Moon Festival. "The most important part of keeping our daughter interested in her heritage is having the whole family involved in it," says Jamie. "Chinese culture is now part of our family's heritage. Our family is richer because of it."

Ryan and Amanda Robbins help their daughter Meera stay connected with India by participating in the India Partnership at their church, by sponsoring a child from India, and by being actively involved in Northwest iChild, a regional support system of 170 families who have adopted children from India.

"Members of the iChild group get together often," says Ryan. The moms go on a yearly retreat to Vancouver, British Columbia— a city that has a large Indian population. The group also hosts a yearly Heritage Day. At a recent Heritage Day, Microsoft's cricket team showed up to demonstrate how one of India's most popular games is played.

Meera looks forward to events such as Heritage Day, says Ryan. "It helps her to better understand her heritage and culture. Best of all, it gives her the opportunity to connect with other adopted kids from India who are in the exact same position she is."

Korean Culture Camp was always a much-anticipated event in Brad and Eileen's household. When Marcus was young, they routinely attended the week-long event with him. "It was great; it showed Marcus other families who looked like ours and it helped him better understand what it means to be Korean," says Brad.

Having a common background and ethnicity with other kids "is no small thing when you're a person of color in a Caucasian family living in a largely Caucasian neighborhood and going to a white majority school," adds Eileen. "The lessons about traditional food, customs, clothing, architecture, music, and games are important because they honor your child's birth country and heritage. But what the kids love most is the intangible comfort of being in a sea of sameness."

Anne Baldwin notes that a child's interest in learning about his birth culture will ebb and flow. "When a child is eight or nine years old and can comprehend abstractly what adoption means and that he is 'different' from his schoolmates, he will likely reject or show no interest in his birth culture." When this happens, give him space, recommends Anne. Continue to provide cultural opportunities for him and "let him know that if and when he's ready to explore his culture, you support that."

In the meantime, don't limit yourself to exploring only your child's culture of origin. Try some of the following cultural enrichment activities:

- Buy a world map. Close your eyes and point to a country on the map. Study that country together, learning about its history, language, folktales, food, and festivals.

- As a family, read news articles about China, Russia, Central America, Europe, Canada, the United States, and your own city.

- Collect nativity sets from different countries and display them at Christmastime.

- Take your child on a short-term mission trip to another country.

When you choose caregivers or teachers for your child, seek out those of several races and cultures. If possible, live in an ethnically diverse neighborhood and attend an ethnically diverse church. As you and your child celebrate a variety of cultures, the tapestry of your lives will become more richly hued.

Different Strokes

Coloring Outside
the Lines

White people don't think much about race. You're white. Big deal. But when you adopt a nonwhite child, everything changes.

As you meander through the mall, proudly pushing a stroller loaded with your brown-skinned child, other shoppers glance at your child and then at you. They do a double-take. As if they're watching a Wimbledon tennis match, their heads swivel back and forth between parent and child, mentally sizing up the mismatched family.

Many smile and nod. Some remark, "What a beautiful child," in an effort to:

a. Cover their confusion.

b. Prove they're comfortable with mixed-race families.

c. Ferret out why white adults are parading around with a brown child.

d. All of the above.

A few bold souls ask, point-blank, "Did you adopt?"

Still others inquire, "Are you babysitting? Where are this child's parents?"

Those who stop to chat nearly always end up asking the million-dollar question: "What is he?"

You smile sweetly and reply, "He's a child."

Public Spectacle Number One

When you adopt transracially, you begin to think about race. A lot. Heather Williams's decision to adopt exposed some internal racial prejudices she hadn't known existed. As she and her husband Matt were deciding "what kind" of child to adopt, Heather told Matt she'd adopt a white or Latino child, but not an African–American.

"I grew up in the South and had deeply entrenched views that said, 'That's Them and this is Us.' I constantly wondered: *What will my family think if we adopt a black child? When people see me with my child, will they imagine I slept with a black man? Will other moms ignore me because I have a black child? What will folks in the grocery store think? Will we be a public spectacle?*"

Heather was stunned when she and Matt received a call from their caseworker, asking whether they'd be interested in adopting a newborn black girl. "The day you get 'the call' is supposed to be the happiest day of your life," she reflects. "You're supposed to be jumping up and down, screaming, 'The baby's coming!' Instead, I felt like a heavy weight was pressing on me. This child wasn't at all what I had expected."

Matt challenged Heather, "What if God was standing here, offering you a present? If you looked at the present and it wasn't what you thought it would be, would you turn it down?"

Suddenly, Heather realized the only thing holding her back from adopting a black baby was the "ugly, yucky pride" of racism. "My worst fear was that our family would stick out, and I didn't want us to stick out," admits Heather. She searched her Bible for verses that addressed racism and discovered God doesn't show favoritism and commands us not to, either. As she studied the book of 1 John, Heather's obsession with earning the approval of others came to light:

> Practically everything that goes on in the world—wanting
> your own way, wanting everything for yourself, wanting

to appear important—has nothing to do with the Father. It just isolates you from him…The person who refuses to love doesn't know the first thing about God, because God is love…If anyone boasts, "I love God" and goes right on hating his brother or sister, thinking nothing of it, he is a liar. If he won't love the person he can see, how can he love the God he can't see? The command we have from Christ is blunt: Loving God includes loving people. You've got to love both.[1]

After asking God to renew her from the inside out,[2] Heather agreed to pursue the adoption. As she and Matt waited for the necessary paperwork to be completed, they talked with their daughter's foster mother every evening. "The baby would make cooing and grunting noises over the phone," recalls Heather. "My heart started to attach to her."

Still, Heather vacillated. "The moment I began to feel confident we could do this, doubts would come crashing back." Heather wondered how she was going to care for a black child's hair. She worried about whether she'd be able to help her daughter connect with her African–American heritage.

Finally, the day arrived when Heather and Matt met their daughter in person. The foster mother stepped out of her house, carrying the baby. Offering the tiny bundle to Heather and Matt, she asked, "Would you like to hold your daughter?"

At that moment, the baby's color no longer mattered. A single thought raced through Heather's mind: *What a precious gift.*

A couple of months later, Heather and Matt took their daughter on her first public outing to their favorite hamburger joint. "There were two black girls behind the counter, looking at our daughter, wide-eyed," recalls Heather. As one of the girls walked out from behind the counter and approached, Heather steeled herself for an interrogation. The girl looked Heather and Matt in the eye and said, "That's a beautiful baby."

As Heather committed to being part of a family that "looks

different," she stepped outside the comfort zone of her tiny, vanilla-flavored world. She prepared to stand out in a crowd, but without the former sense of dread that had plagued her. "People are curious. They ask questions. I use that curiosity as an opportunity to talk about the joys of adoption and about the way God adopts us into His family."

In Living Color

By the middle of the century, it's estimated there will be nearly as many minorities as Caucasians in the United States.[3] When white parents adopt transracially, they cease being a Caucasian family and become a minority family.

When you adopt transracially, you quickly learn to view the world in living color. Simultaneously, you recognize that others see only in black and white. While you feel comfortable with the way your family looks, other people's attention will be drawn to you. When people ask, "Where's your child from?" you must instantly judge the questioner's motives and decide how to respond.

Ryan and Amanda Robbins discovered that most people who ask where their dark-skinned daughter is from are considering adoption or are part of an adoptive family and hope to "talk adoption." Ryan and Amanda give a friendly, succinct response, explaining they adopted Meera from Calcutta, India.

"If the person seems interested, I ask them, 'Are *you* interested in adoption?' with clear emphasis on the *you*. Turning the conversation back on the questioner takes the focus off Meera in a way that often turns the encounter into a positive discussion about adoption," says Ryan.

Ryan and Amanda are regularly questioned about adoption because Meera's younger sister is their Caucasian birth child. "We're often asked whether Meera and Kiera are sisters. I just say, 'Yes, they are,' in a friendly tone. We don't want to send Meera the message that her adoption and her skin color are embarrassing or something

Slurs and Stereotyping

■ ■ ■

Becoming a family of color means readying yourself and your child to encounter racial slurs. Connie Larson, a 24-year-old who was adopted from Korea as an infant, remembers walking into a hardware store with her dad (who's of German descent) when she was a teenager. Another customer saw them coming and remarked, "She must be his concubine."

Lisa, adopted from Korea by white parents, endured racist teasing from her classmates on the school bus. Unwilling to hurt her parents' feelings and fearful that if they knew about the bullying, her parents would make a stink about it and embarrass her, Lisa never mentioned the slights. When she was a teenager, her mom asked her whether other kids in their mostly white community ever gave Lisa a bad time about her adoption or her Korean heritage. "All the time, Mom," she replied.

School-age children often encounter racial stereotyping. Teachers may assign an adopted child from Guatemala a report on Central America; expect a black child to be the school track star; or ask a child adopted from Ukraine to translate for the new Russian student. If this happens, make an appointment with your child's teacher(s), explaining as much about your situation as you feel necessary and pointing out that you do not expect your child to receive "special" treatment.

we need to be secretive about," explains Ryan. "We want her to see us being comfortable with who we are."

Tracee, a Caucasian mom of two biracial daughters, builds humor into her response. When asked what country her girls are from (they were born in Lancaster and Hershey, Pennsylvania), Tracee answers that one child is from "Amish Country," and the other is from "Chocolate Country."

Jarrod, a Caucasian dad with a Latino son, plays dumb when he encounters ill-mannered gossipmongers. When Jarrod is asked, "Where's he from?" he responds, "We live in Detroit. Why are you interested?" This rejoinder flusters most curiosity seekers, who quickly backtrack. Jarrod deflects persistent busybodies by smiling politely and replying, "I'd prefer not to talk about it."

Surviving and Thriving

As your child grows, your job is to train her to survive—and thrive—in a racist world. Talk with her about racism in ways that are age-appropriate. While you don't have to lecture her on the history of racism when she's three, neither should you shield her from the shroud of racism that will veil her life. You should explain that people aren't staring at her simply because she's the cutest child on the face of the earth, but because they notice your family looks different from most. Identify the names your child can expect to be called and help her understand what those taunts imply and why people feel compelled to use them. Together, strategize your responses to racist jokes, dirty looks, insults, and inferior treatment directed at your child or family.

Sheri and Lyle Hatton, who are preparing to adopt a child from Ethiopia, purchased children's books that talk about racism—books that encourage children to develop a strong, positive, confident sense of racial identity. Sheri and Lyle understand they won't be able to protect their child from racial bias, so they're planning how they'll confront it and how they'll help their child work through it.

Brad and Eileen did the same, reading *Chinese Eyes* (by Marjorie

Ann Waybill and Pauline Cutrell) to their Korean-born son as a low-key way to teach Marcus how to respond to teasing.

All the preparation in the world won't diminish the protective instincts that kick into high gear when someone directs a degrading look or epithet toward your child. While it's important to challenge the comment, you can demonstrate mercy while doing so. Three members of Heather and Matt Williams's extended family refuse to attend gatherings in which the Williams' African–American daughter is present. "I want to wring their ever-loving necks," says Heather. "I think of every terrible thing I can say to them." She's considered telling the grandfather, aunt, and uncle: "Forget you! If you don't want to be part of our daughter's life, we won't be inviting you to birthday parties or family get-togethers."

Then God's quiet voice reminds Heather, *Remember how petrified you were to adopt a black child? I showed you grace in helping you change your attitude. Give Me time to work; allow your daughter's grandpa, aunt, and uncle to experience the same grace I extended to you.* So when she feels tempted to rip her relatives' heads off, she calms herself with words from the book of 1 Peter: "Do not repay evil with evil, or insult with insult, but with blessing."[4]

Heather and Matt decided that cutting their relatives off would guarantee they'd continue to live in bigoted ignorance. So she and Matt kept the door open, sending Grandpa pictures and keeping him informed about their daughter's growth and progress. Five days before he died, Grandpa read some Billy Graham materials that convicted him of his misguided prejudice. "He expressed true regret," says Heather. "It was amazing to see how God can soften someone's heart up until their dying day. God's not done with us until we take our last breath."

Bananas, Twinkies, and Oreos

When Sheri and Lyle Hatton decided to adopt an Ethiopian child, they moved to an ethnically diverse area of their city. They are investigating racially diverse play groups and are actively becoming color-aware, rather than color-blind.

Color blindness means never mentioning the fact that your child is a different color than you. It means pretending your child's race doesn't matter. It means assuming that the only thing your child needs to validate her racial identity is your love and acceptance. Color blindness means erasing your child's racial truth. Blindness, writes Jaiya John in his memoir, *Black Baby White Hands,* is a term that implies you do not see something that is there to be seen.

Ignoring your child's racial identity creates a *Banana, Twinkie,* or *Oreo Effect:* Your child is conditioned to act and feel white, but her brown-tinted outside belies her inner self. Her inside and outside don't match.

Jaiya John, an African–American adopted by white parents during the late 1960s, was one of a handful of black faces in a mostly white community. He describes the *Oreo Effect* he experienced:

> The lack of secure and meaningful attachments to other African–American people was a vacuum that bore a hole into the bottom of my self-esteem reserve. Draining steadily out of me was the substance of my positive regard for the person I was…I never wanted my blackness to be nullified, denied, or erased. I just wanted it to be placed in its proper context within the set of characteristics that made up who I was. I wanted my skin color, physical features, and cultural heritage to be appreciated and valued…I needed my family to be the first and last bastion for my racial validation. I needed them to actively plant the seed in me that this racial part of my person was a good thing.[5]

John lived with a black foster mother for the first nine months of his life. During those months and during the months he lived in his mother's womb, John believes he was imprinted with the emotions, rhythms, sounds, voices, and social influx of his black mother and foster mother. He writes,

Culture—more than just holidays and food—is a deeply subtle substance that is with us from birth. It resides in our spiritual inheritance, and is deepened further yet from the moment of conception as we absorb this new, dazzling world we have entered.[6]

When your child is a different color than nearly everyone in her world, questions about her identity will simmer just beneath the surface of your consciousness. Ultimately, your child will decide whether to embrace or reject her ethnic culture, but if you ignore it, she won't have either option. No matter how uncomfortable, no matter how difficult, you must make it a priority to honor your child's ethnic legacy. Many adoption agencies offer courses on racism and cultural awareness as part of their required curriculum for prospective parents. Community centers and adoptive family organizations also frequently offer workshops.

Sheri and Lyle Hatton participate in several online Ethiopian adoption forums. "We talk about different issues and encourage each other," says Sheri. She and Lyle are learning to cook Ethiopian foods and they enjoy eating at Ethiopian restaurants, where they're building friendships with others in the Ethiopian community.

When Brad and Eileen's son was young, he joined a Boy Scouts troop comprised of Japanese–American, Chinese–American, Filipino–American, and Korean–American boys. This melting pot of families representing several cultures was a huge factor in helping Marcus define his Asian–American identity.

Brad encourages all families to find similar groups for their children, whether the organizations are Scouts, drama clubs, sports teams, or church groups. "We had to drive out of our way to get to Scouts every week because the troop was sponsored by a Japanese Baptist Church in another area of our city. But the time commitment was well worth it," he says.

There are several additional ways you can help your child develop a healthy sense of ethnic identity:

- Build friendships with other interracial families.

- Seek out non-exploitive, same-race role models who will regularly spend time with your child.

- Live, worship, and educate your child in an ethnically diverse community.

- Patronize businesses and service professionals of your child's ethnic background.

- Become proficient in hair- and skin-care techniques specific to your child's ethnic background.

- Ask for help from others who share your child's ethnicity.

- Read books, listen to music, attend theater productions, and visit museums and art galleries that showcase your child's ethnic heritage.

- Talk about your child's ethnicity and let her know you'll support her as she forges her ethnic identity.

Rachel and Greg White, parents of twin biracial daughters, take ethnic enrichment one step further: They expose their daughters to experiences from a variety of cultures. They discuss the racism that exists today in our nation with their African–American/Caucasian girls as well as our nation's past struggles with slavery. They also spend at least one week every year visiting their First Nations friends in Canada. Their daughters took a Japanese culture class to honor Greg, who was born in Japan. The family went on a mission trip to Tijuana, Mexico, where the girls met many children their age as they built houses in a barrio area. The family has several close friends who live in Nepal, the Solomon Islands, Kenya, South Africa, and Niger.

"Our cultural experiences are based on relationships with people," says Rachel. "While we try to help our daughters feel comfortable and beautiful in their own brown skin, we also hope to instill in them the ability to see the beauty in other cultures and ethnic groups."

The Born Identity

Color-aware children who are instilled with a sense of belonging to their parents' ethnic community as well as to their own ethnic group feel less racially isolated, develop a less constricted worldview, and possess a healthier self-esteem. As your child grows into her ethnic identity, you can simultaneously affirm her identity as God's beloved child.

In chapter 8 of his letter to the Romans, Paul explains that absolutely *nothing* can get between us and God's love. *Nothing*. Not even people who treat our families as second-class citizens because of our skin tones.

Jesus understands exactly how we feel when others reject or misunderstand us. That's because Jesus was regularly spat on, called "scum," misunderstood, and rejected. This Jesus, God-in-the-flesh, relates to everything we experience because He experienced it, too.

Paul further assures us that God's Spirit walks alongside us, helping us through every trial, every identity crisis. "He knows us far better than we know ourselves," Paul writes. "God's Spirit touches our spirits and confirms who we really are: His children."[7] In *Him* we live and move and have our being.

12

Love Me Tender, Love Me Sweet

When Differences Are
Called "Special Needs"

Ainsley was the picture of health when William and Laura met her at the Chinese orphanage. Nine months old, she looked more robust than the other two babies her age who were being adopted by U.S. families. But Ainsley had less muscle tone and couldn't sit unsupported. "We assumed it was due to a lack of attention and stimulation," says Laura.

Ainsley's adoption referral had noted she was a normal, healthy infant. But when she visited her pediatrician a week after arriving home, Ainsley's doctor was alarmed by the lack of muscle tone in her hips. Fearing her hips might be dislocated, the doctor ordered x-rays, which showed nothing out of the ordinary.

For six months, Laura and William did "floor time" at least twice daily with Ainsley: placing her on her belly, distracting her with toys, and encouraging her to use her muscles to explore her world. But by the age of 15 months, Ainsley showed no signs of learning to walk. Her pediatrician recommended a muscle tone assessment. Again, the results specified nothing serious enough to warrant treatment.

Six months later, she was retested. This time, Ainsley qualified for physical therapy. After working with Ainsley for a couple of weeks, her physical therapist began to suspect she had cerebral palsy, a disorder that impairs movement.

Laura and William visited three more doctors, two of whom concurred Ainsley did, indeed, have cerebral palsy. "The diagnosis threw us for a loop," says Laura. "We had to give up the idea she'll be on the same developmental level as other kids her age."

Now 5 years old, Ainsley wears stylish, multi-colored ankle foot supports (braces) she calls "magic boots." She's had to forgo ballet and soccer, but she may try karate, gymnastics, or ice skating. "She loves monkey bars," adds Laura. "She can roller skate and ride a tricycle and a scooter."

When Ainsley isn't wearing her braces she falls frequently. "Some people give me dirty looks when I don't pick her up, but I don't want to coddle her too much," explains Laura. "Overall, she's doing great. If she'd stayed in China she might not have ever walked. Here, she can get the therapy she needs."

Laura and William have never regretted adopting Ainsley. "I can't imagine life without her," says Laura. "She's intelligent and loving. She makes everything worthwhile. She completes our family."

Detour Ahead

In the adoption world, "special needs" refers to any factor or condition that makes a child harder to place in an adoptive family. Often a child's age, ethnicity, or membership in a sibling group makes her harder to place. A child who has physical, mental, or emotional challenges is also labeled "special needs."

Medical special needs encompass everything from minor, correctable conditions to severe disorders and diseases. For instance, a child classified as special needs might have chronic ear infections, dyslexia, a heart murmur, cleft palate, AIDS, Down syndrome, limb malformations, or Fetal Alcohol Syndrome.

If you're like most parents you probably won't set out to adopt a child with special needs. But as you peruse adoption photo listings, something may draw you irresistibly toward a particular child. Or you might discover your child's existence through a friend who tells you about a three-year-old with a stutter who's waiting to be adopted from foster care. And it's not uncommon to receive a call from your adoption social worker, who says, "I know you specified you want to adopt a healthy child. But I just learned of this sweet little girl who has an extra toe on her left foot. Would you consider adopting her?"

Brett and Laurie Amelung had every intention of adopting a healthy infant girl from Russia. But even after submitting their application to adopt, Laurie couldn't get special needs adoption out of her mind. One day, as she was browsing through a special-needs flyer from her adoption agency, Laurie noticed a grainy black and white photo of an adorable 14-month-old Russian girl who was missing an ear. She felt compelled to investigate.

Developmentally on target, Hannah had been passed over many times because of a congenital ear deformity called *microtia*. After researching her condition and speaking with several specialists who explained the reconstructive surgery Hannah would need, Brett and Laurie felt confident they could handle Hannah's condition. Five months later, Hannah joined the Amelung family and began thriving in her new environment.

During the eight years since Hannah joined her family she has undergone four surgeries. And she's recently been diagnosed with a learning challenge, common among children with microtia. But overall, says Laurie, "She's a normal, bright, vivacious, happy-go-lucky little girl who happens to have been born without an ear."

While Hannah has a profound hearing loss in one ear, Brett notes, "She can still hear the sound of the snack cupboard opening two rooms away." Her "missing ear" is such a small part of the "wonderful, funny, loving girl she is," says Brett. "I'm so glad it didn't keep us from adopting her."

Children with medical special needs are often emotionally healthy, writes Lee Tobin McClain in *Adoptive Families*.[1] As you look at photo listings of children available for adoption, do so with an open mind—you may surprise yourself. Rather than fearing the limits of your ability to love, ask God to nudge your heart open a little further. You may sense God urging you, "This child needs a home, and I've chosen you to parent her. I'll equip you for the task. Are you willing?"

About a year and a half after they adopted Hannah, Brett and Laurie decided to adopt again. "We were firmly convinced we only wanted to consider special needs adoption this time," says Laurie. "It was heartbreaking to know there are so many kids who hardly stand a chance of being adopted just because they have special needs."

They requested to adopt a girl with cleft lip and palate. As often happens when parents indicate they're willing to adopt a child with a specific need, Brett and Laurie's agency alerted them to a second child—also with cleft lip and palate—who needed to be adopted. They said "yes" to him as well, brought both children home from Russia together, and embarked on a hectic round of doctors' appointments, evaluations, therapy sessions, and surgeries.

"Hunter transformed from a malnourished, 14-pound 20-month-old into a healthy, active, engaging little boy," says Laurie. "And Daria grew from a 12-pound 1-year-old with a "very large cleft" into "a beautiful toddler with a bright smile that lights up a room."

Brett and Laurie went on to adopt yet another son, a 7-year-old with the same ear condition as Hannah. "We're grateful God opened our hearts to special needs adoption," says Laurie. "God has grown us and taught us through them. The rewards of parenting them are far greater than the challenges. We've been blessed so much by taking the detour from the path we had chosen."

Prepare for Launch

When you inform others of your decision to adopt a child with special needs, you're bound to receive interesting feedback. Some will dub you a saint, burbling, "Oh, you're *so* wonderful!"

You'll also encounter skeptics who ask why you'd want to spend your life caring for "damaged goods." When Michelle and Steve

Gardner, parents of three birth children (then 10, 8, and 5), were considering adopting a girl who had a cleft lip and palate, they were told they'd be cheating their birth children by investing their time and money into a special needs child.

They were advised to "take it easy," to coast through parenting rather than starting over with something even more challenging. "One relative said it made him sick to his stomach to think about what we were considering doing to ourselves and our other children," writes Michelle in her book, *Adoption as a Ministry, Adoption as a Blessing.*[2]

Michelle and Steve discussed every imaginable angle about how adopting might affect their family dynamic. They kept coming back to a verse in the book of Matthew: "The King will reply, 'I tell you the truth, whatever you did for one of the least of these brothers of mine, you did for me.' "[3]

Michelle and Steve decided to adopt the girl with the cleft lip and palate. Then they adopted a girl with limb deficiencies. Then a blind boy. Then two children from Ethiopia. Then another girl. Then three more children, bringing their grand total of children to 12. "How much we would have missed if we had listened to our fears," writes Michelle.[4]

Preparing to parent a child with special needs means willingly adjusting virtually every aspect of your life to accommodate your child. In her book, *Empowering Your Child Who Has Special Needs*, Debbie Salter Goodwin advises,

> Your child's ongoing special needs will change how you live and where you live. They change vacations. They change leisure activities. They change mealtimes. They affect *everything*. Learning disabilities mean tutoring and extra help with homework. A physical diagnosis means doctors' appointments, watching for symptoms, and often dealing with medication issues. A mental health issue means counseling, learning coping strategies, and balancing medication.[5]

The Support System

■ ■ ■

You will be your child's primary advocate as you work with pediatricians, specialists, social workers, child psychiatrists, caregivers, therapists, insurance providers, and school personnel. You'll need to possess several critical character traits: courage, optimism, willingness to learn, sense of humor, perseverance, creativity, flexibility, determination, and a thick skin. And because parenting a child with medical challenges is physically and emotionally exhausting, you must begin assembling a support system *before* you adopt your child.

- Learn whether the medical, educational, mental health, and social services that exist in your area are equipped to handle your child's needs. Ask about their experience working with adopted children.

- Visit support groups specific to your child's need and ask the parents who attend how the group benefits their family.

- Contact adoption agencies in your area that specialize in the placement of children with special needs. If they offer a post-adoption support program, ask if you can attend, regardless of whether you adopt through their agency.

- Contact your health insurance company and learn exactly what your policy covers in regards to your future child's specific needs.

- Alert your employer you'll need to take time off

to attend medical and therapy appointments with your child. Consider negotiating a flexible work schedule, changing your shift, working part time, or telecommuting.

- Meet with extended family members, close friends, and those in your faith community. Explain the needs you anticipate your child will have and enlist their help.

- Meet with an estate planning attorney to designate a guardian and a health care plan for your child should you pass away.

- Look into counseling for yourself. Adopting a child with medical challenges will wreak havoc on your emotional and spiritual health and can damage your relationship with your spouse, your other children, and friends. Interview several psychologists or counselors so you'll have a good sense of who will be a good fit for you when the time comes.

- Schedule downtime for yourself, both during the adoption process and after your child arrives in your family. You'll feel tempted to devote every ounce of energy to your child. Don't. Save some energy for yourself, and if you're married, reserve some energy for your spouse.

The best gift married couples can give their special-needs child is a strong marriage, says Goodwin:

> Do whatever it takes to make time for each other. Hire a sitter, check out respite care, use a baby monitor, or lock a door. Plan how you'll reconnect with each other at the end of a busy day. Don't stop talking to each other about your dreams, your days, or your fears. Don't stop having fun with each other. Time invested in each other is not selfish—it's a life-saving activity for all of you.[6]

Three...Two...One...Blastoff!

Beth and Sam agree a strong marriage truly is life-saving. Daily, they're pushed to their physical, emotional, and spiritual limits as they parent two children with special needs. In 1997, when they adopted five-year-old Anne and four-month-old Stephen from Russia, they expected their children to be developmentally delayed. But developmental delays turned out to be the least of their worries.

Two days before they left for Russia, Beth and Sam received their daughter's height and weight information; she scored below the second percentile on both grids. When they met Anne, she was verbally non-responsive. Still, U.S. doctors believed Anne would "catch up" with her peers in both growth and language development.

That hasn't happened. Anne, now a teenager, struggles with severe language limitations and is in the twenty-fifth percentile for height and weight. Four years after joining Beth and Sam's family, Anne was diagnosed with Fetal Alcohol Syndrome (FAS). Resulting from prenatal exposure to alcohol, FAS is a lifelong condition that causes physical and mental disabilities.

Their son Stephen was diagnosed with motor skills challenges and Attention Deficit Hyperactivity Disorder (ADHD).

Receiving a definitive diagnosis of Fetal Alcohol Syndrome was a relief for Beth and Sam, who for years had agonized about Anne's lack of impulse control. Soon after Anne joined their family, Beth suspected something was seriously wrong with her daughter so she researched fetal alcohol exposure and attachment disorder. One of Beth's friends, a foster parent, told her Anne's symptoms mirrored those of foster children whose mothers were addicted to drugs and alcohol.

Beth began recording every instance of behavior she considered out of the ordinary. Then she took Anne to a Fetal Alcohol Syndrome clinic for an evaluation. After several days of testing and interviews, the doctors diagnosed Anne with FAS, based on her physical and psychological symptoms.

The diagnosis explained Anne's tiny size and language challenges. It explained her inability to entertain herself for even a few minutes at a time. It explained her urge to constantly run, screaming, through the house. It explained her compulsion to climb all over people and rub her body against theirs. It explained why it took three adults to hold down the 30-pound spitfire when giving her immunizations. It explained why she required anesthesia when receiving dental fillings. It explained Anne's extremely narrow palate that requires extensive orthodontic work. Perhaps most importantly, the diagnosis helped Beth and Sam realize they weren't terrible parents and Anne wasn't a terrible kid. Anne's behaviors were a result of something neither she nor her adoptive parents could control.

■ ■ ■

Beth wishes she had known the symptoms of FAS earlier. "It would have spared us a great deal of frustration and self-doubt concerning our parenting abilities." Before Anne's diagnosis, when Beth and Sam were struggling to manage their daughter's behavioral issues, well-meaning friends assured them, "Just love her; she'll be fine." Those same friends rarely invited Anne to parties or outings.

Beth reflects, "Can I blame a mom for not wanting her daughter's birthday party to become a chaos zone?"

For Beth, parenting two children with special needs has often been lonely, particularly when Anne was younger. "I wanted to become a recluse but since my husband is a pastor, I didn't have that option. At church, I would paint a smile on my face and then burst into tears the minute I arrived home."

Several people from her church kept her out of the insane asylum, Beth believes. One mom invited Anne over for play dates with her daughter and closely monitored the girls to ensure everyone was having a good time. A speech therapist visited weekly, just because she knew Anne needed help. A grandmother of two foster grandchildren loved and accepted Anne and Steven, celebrating every inch of their progress.

Still, the constant struggles and heartache of parenting children with difficult challenges wore on Beth and Sam. Sam experienced a particularly dark period in his job as pastor of a new church. As his children's needs increased, he devoted less attention to the needs of those in his church. Beth, too, was unable to allot much time or energy to ministries within the church. Church members began offering "friendly advice" to Sam and Beth—advice that indicated they expected more from their pastor and his wife. "When it routinely took every ounce of strength we could muster to go to church on Sunday, we knew it was time for us to leave," says Beth.

Sam resigned from his job and they sold their house, bought a motorhome and hit the road for six months. "During that time, I homeschooled Anne (then eight) and was in close proximity to her 24/7," says Beth. "Anne made great strides in her ability to speak and write and we worked consistently on behavioral issues. We began to see small signs of attachment."

Beth believes the road trip was the best decision she and Sam ever made for their family. "Sam and I began to learn what worked and what didn't. Gradually, we lost the feeling of hopelessness and helplessness. We literally needed life to stop in order to know how to go on."

Go on they do, one day at a time. While the challenges continue, there are plenty of encouraging signs. Anne, who derives comfort from routine, functions "quite nicely" in structured situations. She now shows remorse when she's misbehaved—a trait that didn't exist during her first four years in the family. She has begun to share her frustrations at school with her parents and she sheds genuine tears, a significant milestone for a girl who, until recently, feigned emotion. Anne has also discovered a passion for writing. "She'll spend hours typing away, communicating stories too difficult for her to synthesize orally," says Beth.

Daily, Beth becomes more convinced of God's grace. While she and Sam have felt pushed to their personal limits, she believes overall, the experience has strengthened their marriage. And Beth delights in her children. "My kids make me laugh. They enrich my life, brighten my days, and teach me about myself. I have the added benefit of knowing I have been used by God to love children who might have otherwise known despair." Life is definitely not hopeless for Beth and Sam—or for their children.

Treated Like a Prince

One of my favorite Bible stories offers hope for parents who are considering adopting a child with special needs. The story features a medically challenged boy named Mephibosheth (me-FIB-uh-sheth).

Mephibosheth was the grandson of Saul, Israel's first king. Saul was impulsive, rarely listening to God and serving Him only half-heartedly. His attitude grieved the Lord, who decided to appoint a new king who truly loved and obeyed Him.

Enter David. You're probably familiar with the classic underdog vs. superpower matchup in which the "apple-cheeked, peach-fuzzed" shepherd boy slings stones at the nine-foot-tall Philistine champion, Goliath. Young David's heroics don't sit well with King Saul. Consumed with jealousy, Saul spends the remainder of his 42-year reign seeking opportunities to kill David.

David's best buddy, Jonathan (who happens to be Saul's son), is ashamed of his dad's behavior towards David. Fearful Saul's jealousy will result in the demise of the royal family, Jonathan begs David,

"If I die, keep the covenant friendship with my family—forever." David agrees, and the two swear eternal friendship.

Fast-forward to the last day of Saul's life. At age 72, Saul is still battling those pesky Philistines. The Philistine archers kill Jonathan and critically wound Saul, who proceeds to take his own life. At this point, Mephibosheth makes his appearance. When the news about Saul and Jonathan reaches the royal household, Mephibosheth's nurse scoops the five-year-old boy into her arms and runs. In her hurry to escape the royal residence, she drops Mephibosheth, and both his feet become crippled.

The disabled boy escapes to the land of Gilead, where he grows up in the household of a man named Makir. Meanwhile, David, now king of Israel, has been busy conquering bad guys. One day, he begins reminiscing about his friend Jonathan. David wonders, "Is there anyone left from Saul's family? If so, I'd like to show them kindness, in memory of the promise I made to Jonathan all those years ago."

That's when David learns Jonathan has a son. He can't wait to see Mephibosheth, and he summons him immediately to Jerusalem. Mephibosheth limps into David's presence, trembling.

Seeing the image of Jonathan in the young man's face, David melts. He leans forward and whispers, "Don't be afraid." I imagine David adding, "I loved your father as much as I love myself. And because I loved him, I am going to adopt you!"

Mephibosheth replies, "Who am I that you pay attention to a stray dog like me?"

David shifts in his chair and considers Mephibosheth's question. Yes, Mephibosheth is disabled. His social status is lower than a stray dog's. He probably can't get a job. He lives off the charity of others. He has lost his land, his inheritance, and his entire extended family. He is a *nobody*.

But not to David. "I'm going to give you back all the land that belonged to your Grandpa Saul, and you're going to eat at my table from now on," declares David. And that's exactly what happens:

"Mephibosheth ate at David's table like one of the king's sons." David restores Mephibosheth's dignity by bestowing on him the highest honor in the kingdom—the honor of dining daily with his adoptive father.[7]

The significance of a father's love is not lost on David. In a conversation with his heavenly Father, David requests one gift from the Lord: "That I may dwell in the house of the LORD all the days of my life."[8] David understands what it's like to be broken, lonely, and afraid. He knows what's it's like to yearn for a safe haven. So, instead of merely thinking kind thoughts about Mephibosheth, David takes action. He seeks out Mephibosheth and welcomes this scarred young man into his family. David considers it a privilege—not a duty—to offer a permanent home to Mephibosheth.

It's easy to imagine David and his new son rejoicing together with the words from Psalm 68: "Sing to God, sing praise to his name...father of orphans...God sets the lonely in families...you are awesome, O God...praise be to God!"

■ ■ ■

God called David "a man after my own heart." In adopting Mephibosheth, David modeled the attitude all who consider adopting a child with special needs can emulate: He committed his life to Mephibosheth because he treasured his friendship with Jonathan and because he wanted to delight God. You, too, will delight your heavenly Father as you celebrate your child's accomplishments and appreciate your child's uniqueness.

Laurie and Brett Amelung, who adopted four children with medical challenges, had 50 doctor appointments and four surgeries during a two-month period. But when people ask them what kind of "problem" their kids have, they respond, "Our children's biggest problem is they are normal, naughty, fun, fabulous, ornery kids." Yes, their family sees a few more specialists than the average family. Yes, their kids have undergone a total of 20 surgeries among them so far. And yes, Laurie and Brett shuttle their children to speech therapy, occupational therapy, and physical therapy. But overall, they say they're just an average family. "An average family with some special kids."

"Life empowered by God is never disabled," writes Debbie Salter Goodwin. As you commit to adopting one of God's special children, inhale encouragement from the words of 1 Samuel: "Men and women look at the outward appearance, but the LORD looks at the heart."[9]

My DNA Made Me Do It

During his first day of kindergarten our son Ben got sent to the principal's office for turning off the restroom lights on a fellow student. While Ben enjoyed the opportunity to socialize with the principal, the incident humiliated Robert and me. Robert's only trip to the principal was to learn he'd received a college scholarship, and I'd never served a day of detention in my life.

"I didn't sign up for this," I wailed.

Robert and I had hoped our children would do well in school. For us—teachers with master's degrees in hand—*doing well* meant our kids would come equipped with above-average IQs and a yearning to soak up knowledge. Yes, we were education snobs.

But God had a sneaky plan to rid us of our snobbery—He sent us two sons who face learning challenges. In the years since Ben and Josh started elementary school, Robert and I have gotten to know school personnel with whom we rarely interacted during our pre-parenting days: psychologists, therapists, resource-room teachers, and of course, the principal. These folks helped us understand that while our sons learn differently than the majority of the school population, they are, indeed, *doing well.*

When Josh was assigned his Big Fourth-Grade Project—the salt-clay relief map of our state—he decided he'd rather build it out of

Legos. Thousands of Legos later, our petite son tottered into his class-room, carefully balancing his 13-pound, 3-foot wide scale model of Washington state constructed entirely of Legos (it's times like these I wish we lived in Rhode Island). It came as no surprise when Josh informed us he's planning to be an "art-i-tech" when he grows up.

While my sons aren't bookworms and they struggle to pass the statewide student-assessment test, they're smart in ways I will never be. Josh charms everyone he meets with his easygoing nature and sweet spirit. Ben, who began his school career in the principal's office, won the most prestigious honor awarded during his sixth-grade graduation—the award for "unselfish thinking of others." He can pitch a wicked changeup from the baseball mound, and he's a genius at finding the open man on a basketball court. At the end of seventh grade, he won an "academic" award for "Outstanding P.E. Student."

These two boys, who are so different from Robert and me, are the true educators in our family. They are living examples of God's workmanship, created to exhibit the unique characteristics with which He molded them.

The Superhero Syndrome Strikes Again

Ben and Josh were robust, good-natured babies. As they grew, atypical behaviors and developmental deficits began to emerge. I wondered: *Just how much of my children's behavior can I attribute to adoption? Are their struggles a result of poor genes, poor parenting, or are they a fluke of nature?* The statistics worried me:

- More than 30 percent of adopted children have a learning or attention problem.[1]

- Between 40 and 80 percent of foster children have sig-nificant mental-health problems.[2]

- More than 800,000 children with severe attachment disorder come to the attention of the child welfare system each year. This figure does not include thousands of children with attachment disorder adopted from other countries.[3]

- Adopted children are ten times more likely than their nonadopted peers to be at risk for psychosocial maldevelopment.[4]

Unwilling to hover over our sons or to attribute every quirky behavior to adoption-induced damage, we stalled. Much of my own reticence to seek professional advice harkens back to the Superhero Syndrome—that urge to prove I was the World's Best Parent. Like many adoptive parents, Robert and I were older than your average first-time parents. We were highly-educated professionals. We'd watched friends and relatives blunder through parenting and had vowed to avoid their mistakes. We would be better, stronger, faster. After passing our home study with flying colors, we felt prepared. Donning our Superhero capes, we leapt into parenting.

There was only one hitch. Our pre-adoption training had prepared us to *get* a child; it hadn't prepared us for what to do *after* we got a child. When relatives not-so-subtly suggested we have our sons tested, Robert and I protested, "They're just fine." Irritated at their interference, we wrote off their advice, thinking they were blowing our children's issues out of proportion.

We were wrong. (Oh, how I hate admitting that!) Looking back on our refusal to face reality, I now understand that pride in our ability to handle everything ourselves kept us from seeking help sooner. It wasn't until our boys reached second grade and their teachers strongly urged us to have them tested that we took action. By the end of their respective second-grade years, each boy had been diagnosed with learning differences (politically correct folks don't call them "learning disabilities" anymore, I've been informed).

Nothing can prepare a parent for hearing the words, "Your child has Post-Traumatic Stress Disorder." Or, "Your child has an attachment disorder"...or ADHD...or auditory processing disorder...or a psychotic disorder…or any of the dozens of disorders and dysfunctionalities that can plague adopted children.

But for Robert and me, learning the names of our sons' challenges brought relief. We'd felt alternately angry, guilty, and melancholy about our sons' "issues." The diagnoses empowered us to stop blaming ourselves, each other, and our children for behaviors none of us had been able to control. As we learned more about Ben and Josh's challenges, Robert and I made appropriate accommodations for our sons, creating an environment that allows them to achieve to their utmost.

Honeymoon's Over

When Kym and Mike began fostering 22-month-old Jake, they expected his incredible busyness, explosive meltdowns, and intense anger to present challenges. But their caseworkers assured them, "As soon as Jake settles in to your home and bonds with you, everything will be fine."

After a year and a half Kym realized, "Jake *has* bonded with us. These problems are not going to go away." When Jake was diagnosed with Attention Deficit Hyperactivity Disorder (ADHD) and sensory integration disorder, Kym sobbed. "There's a loss of a dream—a change in expectations when you realize your child has significant needs you didn't know about," she says. (We'll hear more of Kym and Mike's story later in this chapter.)

In *Parenting the Hurt Child,* Gregory Keck and Regina Kupecky suggest parents act proactively to investigate the causes of unusual behaviors they observe. While the authors speak primarily to parents who adopt older children, their suggestions apply just as readily to those who adopt newborns. Keck and Kupecky advise,

> Post-placement adjustment does not take a long time, and even if your child is from another country, you can expect that he will begin to fit into your family rather quickly—if he is going to fit in at all. Do not wait for

years of troublesome behavior to pass, assuming that he is "getting used to" your family and culture. A honeymoon phase should not extend into years. If it does, you may be in a terminal phase, which means that what is happening will be going on for a protracted length of time, or perhaps forever.[5]

My friend Cynthia adopted a daughter whom she later learned has significant attachment problems. Her five-year-old is aggressive and violent; she lies incessantly, manipulates others, and is unable to show affection. Cynthia shamefacedly confided she sometimes secretly wishes she could take her daughter back to China. Admitting parenting isn't all she'd dreamed took guts. But for Cynthia, confessing her disappointment was the first step toward healing. Rather than giving in to despair, Cynthia sought specialized psychological therapy for her daughter. Together, she and her daughter are working to build healthy attachments.

Part of the Job Description

■ ■ ■

Absorbing criticism and advice from family, friends, and total strangers who've never experienced the issues you face comes with the territory.

Nicola, whose son has severe behavior problems, gives him bear hugs to calm him during tantrums. Watching her struggle with her screaming son, an acquaintance remarked, "If you'd spank him, you wouldn't have that problem."

Another person, who observed Nicola swatting her son's bottom, advised, "If you'd stop spanking him, you wouldn't have that problem."

When your child has a behavioral disorder, no amount of spanking or lack of spanking will make the symptoms disappear. Parenting techniques that work for "normal" children won't work for you. It's good to simply accept that fact.

Meeting the Challenge

Parenting a child who's considered "at-risk" due to psychological disorders, behavioral disorders, or learning differences is demanding, even when your child's challenges are mild. Though you're not responsible for the traumas your child experienced prior to living with you, you *are* responsible for doing what you can to alleviate them.[6]

"It's so important for parents to be prepared and patient," says Kym, mother of 12-year-old Jake and his 19-year-old half sister, Meghan, both of whom have bipolar disorder (a long-term illness characterized by dramatic mood swings and severe changes in energy and behavior).

Kym and her husband, Mike, began fostering their children when Meghan was 9 and Jake was 22 months old. As Meghan entered her teens, she began acting increasingly depressed. "We didn't know how much of her mood swings and crying was due to her being a teenager or to her difficult background," says Kym. But as soon as she and Mike realized Meghan didn't have the ability to pull herself out of her depression, they sought help.

Suspecting bipolar disorder, Meghan's psychiatrist prescribed medication. The medication caused such a dramatic upswing that Meghan decided she didn't need to take it anymore. She went off her medication and her life fell apart. "One day she cried for 24 hours straight," recalls Kym.

Kym and Mike could do nothing to force Meghan to take her medication; in their state, children age 13 and older have the right to make decisions concerning their medical, mental health, and reproductive treatment.[7] "When your child has mental illness, that complicates things," says Kym. Meghan ultimately could decide for herself which medication to use and whether she wanted to take it.

Kym advises parents of teens with mental disorders to discuss the medical consent issue with your child when the teen is in a good frame of mind. "Ask your child to sign a document allowing you access to his or her medical information." Kym also recommends: "Accompany your child into the exam room during medical visits. If you're in the room with your child, you'll have access to any information relayed in that room."

In an attempt to protect Meghan from herself, Kym and Mike responded to Meghan's erratic behavior by enforcing stricter boundaries. "We didn't leave her alone because we were scared she'd try to hurt herself. We told her she couldn't see her boyfriend anymore. But she'd climb out of the window at night, desperate to be with her boyfriend."

In retrospect, tightening the parental screws on Meghan probably wasn't the best decision, reflects Kym. "Meghan had been in several foster care placements and she felt as if she had no control over whom she lived with, whom she loved, or whom she lost. She was functioning at such a place of hurt and loss—compounded by the chemical imbalance—that she couldn't make logical choices."

Faced with the prospect of losing her boyfriend, Meghan decided to take control for the first time in her life. At age 17 she left home, moved in with her boyfriend, got pregnant, and married him. Now 19, Meghan is managing a life over which she has control. And while "she still makes some impulsive choices," says Kym, she's "doing better."

Meghan now tells her mom, "I finally understand what you were trying to protect me from."

Chaos Unleashed

While parenting Meghan has been a roller coaster ride, Kym says raising Jake is even more demanding. When Jake was a toddler, Kym began working full-time, but as things began unraveling with her kids, she wrestled with whether she should work part-time. A Bible verse kept popping into her head: "Whoever welcomes a little child like this in my name welcomes me."[8]

"I felt as if God was saying, 'This little one—Jake—is the mission

I've given you. Put aside your other lofty goals and focus on welcoming this little one in my name.'"

During Jake's preschool years Kym worked part-time off and on
but says it was tough finding a day care that could handle his behavioral issues. When he was four, Jake crawled under the deck of his
day-care center and escaped.

When Kym came to pick him up later that day he informed her,
"This day care is terrible. They lose kids."

"Who did they lose?" asked Kym.

Jake replied, "Me!"

Kym placed Jake into another day care so she could finish up
a two-week substitute teaching job. "I explained all his behavioral
issues to the caregiver." The caregiver nodded and said she could
handle them. After a week, the caregiver called and said she couldn't
keep Jake anymore.

At one point, Kym enrolled Jake in a state-funded therapeutic
preschool program two hours a day, three days a week. "It was a life-
saver for me because it gave me a bit of a break," she says.

Jake began kindergarten in the Christian school where Kym
worked and lasted only two weeks there. "No Christian schools
will take kids that have Jake's problems," she says. "The teachers
aren't equipped to handle them."

Through second grade, Jake was enrolled in a self-contained
public school class for kids with behavioral challenges. "It was a well-
structured program and he had a fabulous teacher," says Kym.

But then her school district made some changes Kym and Mike
knew would negatively impact Jake's progress, so Kym homeschooled
Jake during third grade. "By the end of that year, I was so tired I
decided to put him back in public school," she says.

Midway through his fourth-grade year, Jake's behavior problems
escalated. Mike asked Kym if she'd consider homeschooling Jake
again. "Please, no!" protested Kym.

But she did homeschool him again, and immediately she and

Mike noticed "huge improvements," both academically and behaviorally.

Special Education

Attending church posed additional challenges. "Kids with behavioral issues really stand out at church, where most children are reasonably well-behaved," says Kym. "We couldn't put Jake in the nursery because he would hit the other kids."

When Jake was old enough to attend Sunday school, Kym got called out of every single worship service to deal with him. During the rare moments Kym spent in the service she'd sit and cry because she was so exhausted and overwhelmed. "It got to the point where I didn't want to go to church," she admits.

The family switched churches when Jake was four, joining a small one where they felt they could build relationships. The cycle repeated itself there. One day, when a teacher informed Kym how difficult Jake was, Kym's last vestige of patience snapped. "I am tired of the fact that my child is never welcomed in church," she retorted. "Thank God he's growing up in a Christian family instead of a crack house."

Deciding people at church needed to learn to adapt a little, Kym began educating her child's teachers. "Let's be glad Jake's here, learning about God," she suggested. She and Jake's teacher attended a class together to learn how to work with special needs children. "I was so touched she wanted to learn how to come alongside him," says Kym.

For several years, Kym taught Jake's Sunday-school class. "They called me in every week, so I thought I might as well teach the class," Kym says, chuckling.

When her daughter was 17 and pregnant, church again felt awkward. "What does everyone think of us?" Kym wondered. She found out when her friends from church threw a glamour shower for her. "It was their way of saying, 'We stand with you.'"

Balancing your children's privacy and their need for specialized attention can be tricky, says Kym. "You want to honor your kids by not revealing the details of their life story, but you also have to educate people. Otherwise, they'll wonder why your kid is always misbehaving."

She and Mike decided to openly share their situation. "Most people in our church know about Jake's challenges. Now, at church, I feel totally loved, totally accepted. The people who interact with my kids really try hard to make it work," she adds.

In *Empowering Your Child Who Has Special Needs*, Debbie Salter Goodwin warns parents not to set unreasonably high expectations of volunteer help from within your faith community. "Don't expect the church to do what it doesn't have resources or personnel to do,"[9] she advises.

Still, it's vitally important to remain in fellowship with those who share your faith. Contact your church and ask whether they want to help and have the ability to assist you. Request a recording of the service for those weeks when you're too frazzled to attend. If you enjoy participating in Holy Communion but rarely have the opportunity, ask your pastor or a church elder to serve it to you at your home.

Some churches organize specific ways to support special-needs families, writes Goodwin:

> They may offer a Christian support group. They may have a Sunday School class for children who function better in a context structured to meet their needs. Some offer various kinds of respite care. Others have camps, latchkey programs, or other special activities for children or their parents.[10]

Once the members of your faith community become aware of your family's needs, they will equip themselves to assist you. As you graciously accept their help, not only will your child and your family benefit, but the lives of all who invest themselves in your child will be enriched. Together, you can encourage one another with the same words Paul, Silas, and Timothy used in their letter to the Christians in Thessalonica:

> Every time we think of you, we thank God for you. Day and night you're in our prayers as we call to mind your work of faith, your labor of love, and your patience of hope in following our Master, Jesus Christ, before God our Father. It is clear to us, friends, that God not only loves you very much but also has put his hand on you for something special. When the Message we preached came to you, it wasn't just words. Something happened in you. The Holy Spirit put steel in your convictions.[11]

Joy in the Journey

Although the road has been bumpy, Kym thanks God every day for the opportunity to raise her children. "If they hadn't come to live with us, they would have grown up in really difficult environments," she says. "We've gotten to see their successes."

Their children's successes might seem insignificant to someone outside the family. But for Kym and Mike, the little things their children accomplish are cause for rejoicing. "Jake constantly comes up with creative ideas. He has no fear, he's very brave, and he makes us laugh," says Kym.

And Kym's having a ball being a grandma. "Now that Meghan's a mom, I'm seeing some of the things we taught her in action in her life and in her marriage."

Kym says parenting has molded her into a much, much better person. "I'm less selfish, less judgmental, and more compassionate towards others." Together, she, Mike, and the kids continue to work through the hard stuff. "When we face something, we can look back and say: 'If we got through that, we can surely make it through the next thing.'"

Most importantly, Kym and Mike cherish God's faithfulness as they depend on Him for every need. "I can't even recall the number of times where I've been at a complete loss as to what to do. I pray and God gives me an idea for something—and it works," says Kym.

Given the opportunity, she'd do it again. "I know God has called us to do this," says Kym. "And when God calls you to do something and you do it, no matter how difficult it is, there is joy."

Open-Door Policy

What do you say to the people who have just given you their child?

"Thanks—have a nice life" just doesn't cut it.

So when it came time for us to send our first "update" letter to baby Ben's birth parents, Robert and I searched long and hard for words to express our appreciation for them, our compassion for the sorrow we knew they were feeling, and our delight in the six-pound wiggle-worm who anointed us with upchucked formula every few minutes. After drafting multiple computer-generated and handwritten versions of our letter, we carefully selected photos showcasing Ben at his cutest and popped the packet in the mail.

Our "semi-open" adoption agreement specified that neither we nor Ben's birth family share last names or addresses. Our adoption agency served as intermediary for our correspondence, forwarding letters and packages between us.

While Ben's birth father opted not to correspond with us, his birth mother requested as many letters, pictures, and videos as we were willing to supply. For two years we deluged Jen's mailbox with a running commentary of Ben's life. In return, Jen allowed us into her life. Her ten-page, single-spaced letters—printed on fluorescent pink paper—detailed her breakup with Ben's birth father, her problems with her family, and her senior year of high school.

I mentioned the rapid-fire exchange of letters to someone in my extended family, who inquired, "Doesn't keeping in such close contact with Jen prevent her from moving on with her life? Wouldn't it be better for her if you decreased contact or cut it off altogether?"

I hadn't thought of that. I'd assumed the communication had been healthy for Jen. Horrified at my naiveté, I chastised myself for assuming Jen *wanted* contact when maybe she'd just as soon be rid of us. I wondered what Ben's life would look like without Jen's presence in it.

In my next letter, I asked Jen whether our ongoing communication was helping or hurting. Jen replied, "I *love* the contact. Knowing my son is healthy and happy helps me move on with my life."

Reassured by Jen's response, Robert and I discussed the possibility of opening the adoption: "What are we afraid of? Jen's the nicest person in the world. Let's see if she wants to bag this semi-open adoption business and meet us again in person."

Months earlier, our adoption agency had mistakenly forwarded one of Jen's letters with her last name and address printed on it, so we mailed a letter directly to Jen—a letter that included *our* last name and address.

"Receiving that letter was one of the most meaningful events of my life," Jen later told us. "It proved to me I had gained your trust."

The three of us agreed to meet for dinner at a restaurant near Jen's office. During dinner, when Robert and I asked Jen if she wanted to see her son again, she stared thoughtfully at us for several seconds before replying softly, "I'm not sure."

Jen shared her fantasy in which Ben, at age 18, would run toward her in slow motion through a field of daisies, arms outstretched, the orchestral rendition of "Born Free" swelling in the background.

He'd announce, "Hi, I'm your son," and they'd embrace.

Jen admitted she hadn't begun to process the possibility of seeing Ben when he was only two years old.

In a Pickle

A few weeks after our dinner with Jen, we visited Robert's parents, who live in the city where Jen worked. My goal was to help my mother-in-law can dill pickles. Robert and I planned to meet Jen at her office at five o'clock and take her to a local restaurant.

The pickling process took longer than expected and suddenly it was time to meet Jen. My husband was nowhere to be found, so I enlisted my sister-in-law's help. We buckled Ben into his car seat, jumped in the car, and drove to Jen's workplace.

Leaving Ben in the car with my sister-in-law, I zipped into Jen's office, where I explained the pickle dilemma. Then I casually added, "By the way, Ben's out in the car. Would you like to see him?"

Jen's olive skin turned grey. She heaved a few deep breaths and stammered, "Yes, I think I'm ready to see him."

Forgetting we were supposed to be running in slow motion through a field of daisies, Jen and I hurried to the parking lot. With a flourish, I yanked open the back door. There were no orchestral crescendos, only the sound of the radio blaring the traffic report. Ben, still strapped in his car seat, looked up and chirped, "Hi!" while Jen hyperventilated.

"This is so weird," she gasped. "Here he is! He's right here!"

Then I said something I've never regretted. "Would you like to come to my in-laws' house and have dinner there instead of at a restaurant? I'll warn you, there are a bunch of us. We're canning pickles and the kitchen's a wreck, but we'll be having a picnic in the backyard."

Jen took another deep breath and said, "Yes, I'll come."

Minutes later, we pulled into my in-laws' driveway and climbed out of the car, observing the typical Christianson family drama of screaming cousins chasing each other all over the yard. As the adults became aware of Jen's presence, they drifted over to meet her. That day, Jen was welcomed—not just as an acquaintance or as the birth mother of our son—but as a family member. She's been with us ever since.

Isn't Open Adoption…Weird?

■ ■ ■

Before we adopted Ben, if you'd asked Robert and me whether we'd consider opening our adoptions to the level they are now, we would have flatly stated, "No way!"

To this day, when I explain our "extreme open adoptions" to others, they stare at me, and say, "I don't think I could do that."

Many people have the impression that openness in adoption is out of the ordinary—and just plain weird. And yet adoptions in which birth and adoptive families communicate openly are now the norm. Nearly 80 percent of those involved in domestic infant adoption meet or communicate directly with each other, up from 36 percent two decades ago.[1]

While openness is steadily increasing in popularity, continuing contact after the child's birth is not always a valid option. I do not advocate openness when a child has been abused or neglected by the birth parent(s), or when a birth parent abuses drugs or engages in a lifestyle that could expose his or her child to emotional or physical safety risks.

A year after our semi-open adoption morphed to a completely open one, we met Karen and Blaine, the birth parents of our son Josh. Before Josh was born, Jen joined us at a couple of get-togethers with Karen and Blaine. She informally adopted Blaine, dubbing him her "younger brother."

When Ben was four, he was the ring bearer in Jen's wedding. Josh did the honors for Karen and Blaine when they married each other. As the boys have grown, we've enjoyed countless sporting events, holidays, birthday parties, shopping trips, and even a few overnighters with Ben and Josh's birth families. We've come a long way, baby.

Fear Factor

The term *open adoption* makes many people worried. Perhaps you too have heard some of the following rumors—largely unfounded—about openness:

Rumor #1: *The birth parent(s) will want their child back.* Once your child's birth mother sees what her child's life is like with you, she'll think, "I've made a horrible mistake," and she'll take you to court to get him back. Because she knows where you live, she can decide on a whim to kidnap your child during the dead of night and escape to a desert island, never to be heard from again.

Rumor #2: *You'll have to constantly prove to the birth parent(s) that they made the right decision in placing their child with you.* Letters and photos must tout your child's endearing qualities and downplay the negative ones. There can be no hint of marital struggles, depression, financial difficulties, or career challenges. If your child's birth family visits, you must be on your best behavior, demonstrating how

Allowing for Growth and Change

■ ■ ■

No one seems to agree on an exact definition of *open adoption;* the term encompasses a spectrum of scenarios. For some families, it means a one-time meeting between birth and adoptive parents during which they exchange non-identifying information and family history.

For others, it means corresponding for a limited period after the adoption (often through an intermediary).

For still others, it means exchanging regular e-mails, phone calls, letters, visits, or a combination of those.

That's the beauty of open adoption. The fluidity of its definition grants you and your child's birth parent(s) permission to develop a plan that works best for you—one that allows for growth and change.

wonderful your life is and how happy your child is with *you,* the parent best qualified to raise him. In other words, you must be perfect.

Rumor #3: *Needy, demanding birth parent(s) will weasel their way into your life and interfere with your parenting.* Your child's birth mother will call several times a day and make unannounced visits. She'll expect you to parent not only her child, but her. At the same time, she'll expect to play a mothering role to her child. You'll lose your privacy and you'll never have the opportunity to fully claim your child.

Rumor #4: *Openness will confuse your child*—he won't know who his *real* parents are. Uncertain about whether he's allowed to love both his adoptive parents and his birth parent(s), your child will suffer a perpetual identity crisis. Worse yet, he might idolize his birth parent(s) and decide he likes them more than he likes you.

As you unearth the root of your own fears you'll discover, as Robert and I did, that your anxiety about openness will lessen. Let's take a closer look at the four most common concerns about openness.

Reclamation Project

Birth parent(s) will want their child back. As our relationship with Jen and her husband Isaac was developing, we encountered a situation in which it was advantageous for Jen and Isaac to borrow our car—with Ben in it. As Jen and Isaac drove off with our young son, Robert looked at me with sudden awareness and said slowly, "Do you realize what we just did?"

I gazed at our rapidly disappearing minivan. "We let them take our car—and Ben."

Robert shrugged. "I hope they aren't headed for Canada."

Even after years of loving and trusting Jen, a tiny ember of fear burned. I have yet to meet an adoptive parent who hasn't, at one time or another, harbored misgivings they'll be forced to return their child. Knowing that less than 1 percent of birth parents contest their child's adoption makes no difference.[2] Knowing that a birth parent's chances of reclaiming his or her child are slim to none once the adoption is finalized makes no difference. The fear is so deep-seated, so prevalent, even a world-renowned statistics-spewing authority stands no chance of quashing it.

I began coming to terms with my fear when I tried to view adoption from a birth parent's perspective. Birth parents who have not been coerced into making an adoption plan—those who intentionally choose to place their infant in an open adoption—expend a huge amount of emotional energy screening prospective parents, interviewing them, and nurturing a friendship with them (often for several months before the baby's birth).

In addition, the extensive pregnancy counseling many birth parents receive helps them work through the short- and long-term ramifications—for themselves and for their child—of parenting versus adoption. In short, the majority of birth parents who choose open adoption make a thoughtful decision to which they are strongly committed.

After their baby is born, birth parents are granted a state-mandated waiting period ranging from 48 hours to six months (depending on the state) during which they can revoke their consent to the adoption. This revocation period is the most frightening time of the entire process for adoptive parents. But birth parents who have the opportunity to thoughtfully evaluate whether they feel at peace with their decision are less likely to contest the adoption later.

It's normal for birth parents involved in an open adoption to wonder what life would have been like had they opted to parent their child. But wondering "what if" doesn't necessarily indicate they think they've made the wrong decision. I've often asked Jen whether she wishes she had Ben back. She responds with a laugh, "I like to borrow him for a while, but I'm always happy to return him."

She adds more defiantly, "I made a responsible decision for my child. I placed him with a family I knew would love him, take care of him, and raise him in the way I would want to but was incapable of doing at that point in my life. Why would I go back on my decision?"

Josh's birth father, Blaine, echoes Jen's sentiment. "I wonder all the time what it would be like to parent him," he admits. "But I would never go back on my word. I could never do that to Robert and Laura."

Josh, too, is mystified by the idea of his birth parents reclaiming him. "It would be odd, when you're ten years old, for your birth parents to want to take you back," he reflects. "I have a life with another family. If Blaine and Karen tried to kidnap me, I'd say, 'Get under control!'"

Lights, Cameras, Action!

You must impress your child's birth parent(s). Let's face it; birth parents relinquish their child because their lives are out of synch. They have issues. Heavy issues. They choose adoption because they've experienced dysfunctional relationships. They choose adoption because they're battling physical, emotional, psychological, or financial challenges they feel ill-equipped to handle or want to avoid passing along to their child.

The people who choose you to adopt their child sense qualities in you they hope their child will emulate. They trust you to recognize their child's challenges and provide him with the resources to help him overcome those challenges.

Birth parents have usually endured less-than-perfect home lives; their first exposure to competent parenting skills may be the ones you demonstrate with their child. They are watching you, not to criticize you but to learn from you. They admire you, but they certainly do not expect perfection. In fact, your child's birth parents may feel pressured to present a perfect front to *you*, fearing if they don't, you'll unceremoniously boot them out of your life.

You, on the other hand, may feel as if the birth parent(s) are scrutinizing your every move, waiting to swoop in for the kill at the first sign of weakness. You've just spent several months proving to the world and to the people who chose you to raise their child that you'll be a great parent. It's only natural that you feel pressured to put on an Academy award-winning performance whenever you're in contact with your child's birth parent(s). If you have issues, your first response is to hide them, quick. After all, you don't want to give your child's birth parent(s) the slightest excuse to demand their child back.

While you can effectively disguise your own issues (not that it's a good idea), it's harder to cover up your child's imperfections. When your child launches into a temper tantrum in front of his birth mother, it's a bit tricky to laugh it off by shaking your head in wonder at his antics and mumbling, "He he...I've never seen him do anything like that before."

Meanwhile, you're cringing inwardly and mentally moaning, "She must think I'm a terrible mother!"

While you're busy worrying about what a horrible parent you are, your child's birth mother is probably thinking, "Whew, I'm glad I don't have to deal with *that*. He reminds me of myself when I was that age!"

There's no reason to pretend you're a perfect parent—or that your child is a perfect child—in their presence. When I stopped playing the perfect parent around Jen and shared some of Ben's mysterious personality quirks with her, she nodded in understanding. "Oh yeah, I'm just like that too. If you react this way, it'll backfire...here's what you do..."

Once I worked up the courage to admit parenting perfection escaped me, my son's birth mom became my most reliable adviser, my biggest cheerleader, and my most treasured friend.

Treat Me Right

Your child's birth parent(s) will interfere with your parenting. If you and your child's birth mother meet early in her pregnancy, you might attend prenatal checkups with her, chat on the phone or visit regularly, and form a sisterhood of motherhood. Because you are actively involved in the birth mother's life before your child's birth, it's natural for her to assume she'll be active in your life after she places her child with you.

Three weeks after we adopted Josh his birth parents called, requesting to visit. "But we haven't had time to get to know Josh yet," Robert and I told one another.

After thinking about it, however, we decided a two-hour visit would hardly interfere with our ability to bond with our three-week-old baby. Besides, Karen and Blaine missed him. They just wanted to love on Josh and make sure he was okay. How could we refuse?

When adoption occurs, the balance of power suddenly shifts. The birth mom no longer holds all the cards; now the adoptive parents are completely in charge. Uncertain about how to negotiate this power shift, some continue on as before, welcoming one another as they would a member of the extended family.

Other adoptive parents covet their newfound control and request several weeks or months to privately bond with the baby. While birth parents are counseled to expect this, they may feel disowned when it happens. Those who have no experience setting healthy boundaries in relationships will struggle during the transition.

As you plan your adoption, anticipate the emotional distress your child's birth parent(s) will feel in the days and weeks immediately following the adoption. If possible, negotiate a tentative action plan with the birth parent(s) *before* the adoption. (Many states require a legally binding communication agreement.) Birth parents involved in open adoptions tend to be exceptionally respectful, mature and thoughtful. When they place their child into an open adoption, they understand that while they will always remain an integral part of their child's life, they will not play a parenting role. As you establish healthy boundaries together, feelings are less apt to get hurt.

American Idol

Openness will confuse your child; he might like his birth parents more than he likes you. When Blaine, Josh's birth father, served in Iraq, he e-mailed us pictures of himself garbed in Army fatigues, carrying an extremely large gun. "Cool!" yelled Josh when he saw the photos. Very few things appeal to a boy more than a monstrous gun.

Every August, Ben's birth mother borrows him for a day to take him school shopping. They go out to lunch, and Jen buys him all kinds of expensive clothes I would never dream of purchasing for a rapidly-growing teenager. They return exhausted, yet glowing.

My sons adore their birth parents. Does it make me jealous? No. Because I know they adore Robert and me too, even though they'd be loath to admit it. In open adoption, your child knows from the get-go he has two sets of parents. His birth parents conceived him, planned for his future, gave birth to him, and continue to love him and root for him. His adoptive parents raise him and they, too, love him and root for him. Kids don't seem at all confused by this concept; it's only adults who struggle with it.

To me, open adoption is less confusing for our sons than the alternative they would have experienced had they grown up in their birth families: breakup of relationships; being shuffled among parents and grandparents; and living with siblings, half-siblings, and step-siblings. In open adoption, where all parties care deeply for one another and are mutually invested in loving their child, confusion is practically nonexistent.

I love the way Betsy Keefer and Jayne Schooler put it in *Telling the Truth to Your Adopted or Foster Child: Making Sense of the Past:*

> In the same manner that parents do not stop loving one child when another one enters the family, children have the capacity to love more than one set of parents. They do not have to stop having feelings about their birth family just because they are part of an adoptive family.[3]

Keefer and Schooler explain that when you allow your child to love his birth family and don't involve him in a "competitive, divisive tug-of-war," your child feels free to love and attach to his adoptive family.[4]

It's fine with me if my sons idolize their birth parents. It's fine with me that their birth parents think their son is the best thing since sliced bread. We choose to look for the best in one another. And together, we believe we are giving our children the best of ourselves.

Yours, Mine, and Ours

During the years Robert and I have nurtured friendships with our sons' birth families, we've learned that successful open adoption hinges on truthfulness and trust.

Truthfulness

Most long-term relationships evolve over a period of years. In open adoption, however, the parties commit quickly and agree to remain faithful to one another during their child's lifetime. The intense relationship throws everyone off balance. And when people's emotions are off-kilter, they tend to act irrationally.

One birth mom, who met regularly with the prospective parents of her baby while she was pregnant, requested they name the child "Andrew." The adoptive parents heartily agreed. But when the birth mom received her first batch of post-adoption photos from her son's adoptive family, she was shocked. Several pictures depicted a huge banner strung across the family's front door that announced: "Welcome home, David!"

"The adoptive parents told me whatever they thought I wanted to hear just so they could have my baby," she said. The birth mom felt betrayed and used.

Because openness has become so prevalent in the adoption world, some parents who are desperate to adopt feel pressured to do "whatever it takes" to get a baby. And that includes lying. Lying defeats the purpose of open adoption. In order for openness to work, adoptive parents and birth parents must never, *ever* make promises they don't intend to keep.

If you agree to send letters and pictures on a set schedule, honor your agreement. If you agree the birth family can visit a certain number of times per year, extend the invitation when the time comes. In the same manner, the birth family should make every effort to communicate or visit at the appointed times. Honoring agreements is particularly important as your child gets older. If either party fails to make contact or show up for scheduled visits, your child may assume either his parents or birth parents don't care about him.

Of course, glitches occur even among the best-laid plans. When you negotiate your communication agreement, take into account that your lives will change. You or the birth family may move, have additional children, or pursue career opportunities that make regular contact difficult.

Your friendship won't always be as intense as it is at first; like any relationship, you may be extraordinarily close for a time and then not have the opportunity to talk for ages. As your child grows, his birth parents may pull back or they may draw closer. As you plan your open adoption, build flexibility into your arrangement, but make truthfulness your cornerstone, being "careful to do what is right in the eyes of everybody."[5]

Trust

All healthy relationships are based on mutual trust. In open adoption, the birth parent(s) initiate trust when they choose you to parent their child. You strengthen the bonds of trust as you share your child with the people who entrusted him to you.

Sharing your child might mean showing him pictures of his birth family and telling him what you know about his biological family history. It might mean encouraging him to draw pictures or write letters to his birth parent(s). It might mean visiting the birth family at their home, your home, or in a neutral location such as a park, mall, or restaurant. It might mean attending weddings, funerals, and graduations together; exchanging birthday and Christmas gifts; or enjoying one another's company during family outings such as camping trips and baseball games.

Sharing your child does not imply co-parenting. While you can nurture the special bond that exists between the birth parent(s) and their child, you are your child's legal parent. You must take the initiative to establish firm, loving boundaries with the birth family. If you feel uncomfortable with members of your child's birth family dropping by without calling or without giving several days advance notice, tell them (preferably *before* the first visit).

If you notice your child's birth mother rolling her eyes at your discipline methods or overriding rules you've established, have a frank talk with her. Feelings may be hurt, but it's better to confront issues as they arise than to stew about them privately and jeopardize your long-term relationship.

Learning to trust a virtual stranger is risky. It helps to remember the relationship between you and your child's birth family isn't about you or them; it's about your child. It's about the way your child's life will be enriched over the course of his lifetime as he soaks up the love and devotion of both his birth and adoptive families.

If you're reluctant to start off with a fully open adoption, take it slowly. It's easier to gradually open an adoption than to jump in with both feet, discover you've made a mistake, and be forced to shut down contact with your child's birth family.

Earnestly seek God's direction as you enter open adoption, praying, "God, I don't know how to negotiate this relationship, but You do. Help!" Trust that God listens and responds. The Bible tells us,

> Trust God from the bottom of your heart; don't try to figure out everything on your own. Listen to God's voice in everything you do, everywhere you go; he's the one who will keep you on track.[6]

As you and your child's birth family learn to trust one another and allow God to guide you, you'll very likely experience a rewarding relationship that lasts a lifetime.

Cotton-Candy Thrills

When Ben was seven, we invited Jen and Isaac to our home, intending to cook them a special pre-Christmas dinner and then visit an 800,000-light display. After popping half-a-dozen top sirloins in the broiler, Jen and I sank onto kitchen chairs and became engrossed in conversation. When I opened the oven door to check on the steaks, smoke billowed out and a choir of six smoke alarms began shrieking in unison.

Jen put her arm around my shoulders. "It's okay," she comforted. "I like my steaks well done."

After choking down our charred steaks, we made a beeline out of our smoky house and into our car, where we drove 40 minutes to the Christmas-light display. Ben and Josh promptly fell asleep in the car and when we arrived at the display, Ben woke up wailing. "My foot is asleep! It tingles! I can't move!"

Then he began whining, "I don't wanna look at Christmas lights…I don't wanna look at Christmas lights!"

Trailing 15 feet behind the rest of us, Ben repeated this phrase in a plaintive voice while we made desperate attempts to distract him. Then, just ahead, we spotted salvation: food.

At the concession stands, we bought huge puffballs of cotton candy, homemade caramel corn, soft pretzels, and hot cocoa. Fortified by the massive intake of sugar, Ben and Josh *oohed* and *aahed* over the exquisite light displays and rode the kiddie circus train, where they growled happily at us from behind the bars of their "cage."

A hayride crowned the evening. As we sat in a wagon pulled by a draft horse, we lustily sang "Jingle Bells."

During the drive home, sighs of contentment filled the car. Our tummies were full. Our hearts were full. *This is family,* I thought.

...For the Bible Tells Me So

I'm Adopted...He's Adopted... She's Adopted...We're Adopted... Wouldn't You Like to be Adopted Too?

The first time I took Josh ice-skating, he spent most of the session splayed on the ice. He'd clomp across the ice for a few seconds, marching as stiffly as a toy soldier. Then, splat! He'd do a face-plant.

After observing this scenario replay itself half a dozen times, I grasped his hand firmly in mine and guided him as we inched along. That worked for about ten seconds, until he tripped.

Next, I tried facing him, skating backward while gently pulling him. That threw us both off balance and we wound up in a wet, tangled heap.

Finally, I stood behind him, reached under his armpits and locked my hands across his chest. With a grunt, I hoisted Josh's little body so his blades barely skimmed the ice, and we glided as one.

"I'm skating! I'm skating!" Josh shouted, as I huffed along, knowing my motherly efforts would result in an excruciatingly sore back. But for the moment, we were skating. Life was perfect.

As Josh and Ben have grown, we've shared countless ice-dancing moments during which we connect readily, profoundly. Love and commitment—rather than genetic ties—lace our hearts irrevocably to one another. Whenever I experience an "ice-dancing moment" with my children, I breathe a silent *thank you* to God, the lead partner who guides our family through the dance of life.

The Original Family Planner

Since the beginning of time God has been busy creating families. The day God created humans, He blessed them: "Prosper! Reproduce! Fill Earth! Take charge!"[1]

A little further on in history, God promises an aging, infertile Hebrew couple named Abraham and Sarah they'll be the father and mother of nations, with descendants as numerous as the stars.[2]

Still later in history, an angel of the Lord informs a Jewish carpenter named Joseph that his fiancée is pregnant with a Spirit-conceived child. Joseph must make a tough choice. Legally, he can denounce Mary and have her stoned for getting pregnant out of wedlock. Or he can marry her and informally adopt the baby as his own. Imagine Joseph's frantic internal debate as he wonders which is more important: biological parentage and societal approval or the chance to nurture and train the child God wants him to parent.

When the angel asks, "Joseph of Nazareth: Deal or No Deal?" Joseph shouts, "Deal!"

While Joseph probably doesn't grasp the full implications of parenting God's son, he likely *does* understand this will be the most noteworthy adoption in history. He accepts adoptive fatherhood with grace, taking on the added responsibility of preparing God's son to shoulder the weight of the world's sins. Joseph instinctively "gets" the nebulous concept all parents eventually figure out: We don't own our children. We merely borrow them for a while as we prepare them for adult life.

The angel instructs Joseph to name his son *Jesus*—meaning *God saves*—because He will save his people from their sins.[3] Because of Jesus' life, death, and resurrection, God invites each of us to become His adopted child, promising us a permanent place in His family.

Permanent Change

In his letters to first-century Christians, the apostle Paul explains how our lives are transformed through spiritual adoption. The people to whom Paul preached were familiar with adoption; it was widely practiced in the Roman Empire during that era. According to Roman law, a father wielded absolute control over his son regardless of the son's age. If a father was disappointed in his biological son's character or skill, he could adopt a boy or an independent male adult who demonstrated the qualities he desired. Childless men with no prospect of male biological offspring also sought to adopt sons.

Adoption was a legal transaction, similar to the transfer of parental rights that occurs in today's adoptions. Two steps were involved:

1. In a ceremony of emancipation, the boy's legal and social relationship to his birth family was severed by means of a symbolic sale. Using copper and scales, as typified all financial transactions, the birth father symbolically sold his son and twice bought him back. The third time he did not buy him back, symbolizing the bonds of possession had been broken.[4]

2. After the "sale," the adopting father presented a legal case for the adoption before a Roman magistrate. In the presence of seven witnesses, the father claimed the man as his son. The adopted son then became heir to his father's title and estate and co-heir with any sons born to his adoptive father after his adoption. If, after his father's death, someone challenged the adoption, one or more of the witnesses would testify to its authenticity.[5]

In Roman culture, an adopted son sometimes held greater prestige and privilege than a birth son. In the eyes of the law, once a person was adopted his old life was completely wiped out. Legal debts were canceled and he gained all the rights of a fully legitimate son in his new family. He was figuratively "born again" into his adoptive family.

In a similar manner, all who accept Jesus as their savior are spiritually "born again" into God's family. During Jesus' teaching ministry, a prominent Jewish leader named Nicodemus wondered how a grown adult could be "born again." Jesus explained that spiritual rebirth means allowing God's presence to touch and transform one's life.

Jesus assured Nicodemus, "God so loved the world that he gave his one and only Son, that whoever believes in him shall not perish but have eternal life."[6]

In the same manner a Roman father symbolically "bought" a son, Jesus "bought" us at the price of His own life. When we invite Jesus to be our savior, He breaks the bonds of our sin and severs us from our old life. In the presence of the God the Father, the Holy Spirit, and a heavenly host of witnesses, Christ claims absolute possession of our heart, and we are reborn into a new life as His adopted child.

In his letter to the church at Ephesus, Paul helps us picture God's delight as He plans our spiritual adoption:

> He chose us in Christ before the foundation of the world
> to be holy and blameless before him in love. He destined
> us for adoption as his children through Jesus Christ.[7]

When Paul refers to God's *children,* he uses the Greek word *huiosthesia (huios* means *a son* and *thesis* means *a placing).* All believers are adopted—placed with their heavenly Father. Adoption is not God's second-best choice for building His spiritual family but rather, His first choice. The apostle John writes,

> How great is the love the Father has lavished on us, that
> we should be called children of God! And that is what
> we are![8]

Permanent Inheritance

The moment we accept Christ's offer to adopt us, our adoption is finalized. There's no home study, no paperwork, no court dates. When we act disobedient and willful (which is most of the time), our

Father corrects us. But we don't have to worry God will dissolve our adoption. He'll never get so disgusted with our behavioral challenges that He'll ship us back to the life we led before He adopted us.

Instead, God assures us He's always there, ready to help: "I'll never let you down, never walk off and leave you." God also promises us that Jesus prays constantly on our behalf; He's always on the job to speak up for us.[9]

Because of our spiritual adoption we anticipate the most phenomenal inheritance imaginable: We get to spend eternity with our heavenly Father, heirs of the same boundless love God bestows on His Son. We enjoy prayerful "post-placement visits" with God, eagerly awaiting the moment we'll run through the door of our eternal home, give our Father a huge hug, and receive our permanent inheritance.

Permanent Family

God doesn't want us to just hang around, waiting for our spiritual inheritance. He commissions us to care for the hungry, the homeless, and the hurting. He places the utmost importance on relationships among family members, specifying that *family* includes more than blood relatives.

In the book of Matthew, Jesus points to His disciples and says, "Look closely. These are my mother and brothers. Obedience is thicker than blood. The person who obeys my heavenly Father's will is my brother and sister and mother."[10]

His statement must have shocked his ancestry-obsessed audience. Rather than focusing on the genetic lineage traditionally passed from father to eldest son, Jesus introduced a radical new family structure, asserting that our heavenly Father trumps our earthly father. Not that our earthly parents aren't important. But Jesus wants us to get our priorities straight. He teaches, "Seek first his kingdom and his righteousness, and all these things will be given to you as well."[11]

The glue that binds the family of God is the unconditional *agape* love that permeates every relationship Christians establish. God

God's Permanent Marker

■ ■ ■

We gratefully acknowledge the love with which God permanently marks our lives as we lavish love on our children. The seeds of our love are planted as we wade through reams of paperwork, meet the people who will give birth to our baby, or squint at grainy photos of an orphaned toddler.

Our love takes root as we gently stroke our child's cheek for the first time. We nurture our seedlings as we accept support from medical specialists, therapists, teachers, extended family, friends, and our faith community. As we alternately weather storms and bask in sunshine, we realize that somewhere along the way, love mysteriously bloomed.

models *agape* in choosing to love us, His children, with a ferocity we can't even wrap our minds around. Paul writes,

> I'm absolutely convinced that nothing—nothing living or dead, angelic or demonic, today or tomorrow, high or low, thinkable or unthinkable—absolutely nothing can get between us and God's love because of the way that Jesus our Master has embraced us.[12]

Jesus demonstrates *agape* love throughout His ministry, even as He is dying on the cross. Looking down, Jesus sees His mother standing near His young disciple, John.

Jesus says to His mother, "Woman, here is your son."

To John He says, "Here is your mother."

John himself tells us: From that moment he accepted Mary as his own mother.[13]

Jesus' final act during His earthly lifetime was creating an adoptive family.

Singing Inside

During the minor crises of everyday life, the intensity of my motherly love strikes me anew. As Josh neared his eighth birthday, he decided he didn't want the big birthday bash he'd been planning for months. Instead, he asked us to take him out for pizza and to his school's country western dance.

On the Big Day, Josh awoke with a bad cold. Exhausted, coughing, and sniffing (but anxious to bring treats for his class-mates), he dragged off to school. Hoping to lift my son's spirits, I delivered a batch of his favorite chocolate-chip cookies to his class-room. Unfortunately, Josh had to cut his classroom party short because he was scheduled to attend speech therapy. "My school party was ruined!" Josh wailed when he arrived home that after-noon.

Stuffed up and headachy, he decided he'd rather stay in bed than attend the school dance. I took Ben to the dance instead, antici-pating we'd celebrate Josh's birthday with a freshly-baked chocolate applesauce cake later that evening. When Ben and I returned from the dance, we discovered our cat had licked some of the frosting off Josh's cake. Noticing the crater in his cake, a distraught Josh cried, "The cat ate my birthday cake!"

As we attempted to calm Josh the phone rang. It was his birth parents, informing us they planned to drop by the next day. The tears welled up again. "I haven't had time to prepare for their visit," Josh moaned. While Josh dearly loves Karen and Blaine, their sur-prise announcement superheated his emotional meltdown.

My heart went out to my precious son, who had spent the pre-vious year imagining the perfect birthday only to have everything fall to pieces on the Big Day. But we made it through. We've sur-vived many catastrophes, major and minor, since then.

As our family "grows up" together, I've discovered that I learn at least as much from my sons as they learn from me. One day, when our family was driving home from church, I remarked that I'd been unable to sing during the worship service because I had a hoarse voice from bronchitis.

Josh responded, "Mom, you should sing the words inside your brain like I do. God can still hear you singing, even when you're singing inside your head."

Josh was right. God hears every song, every prayer. God loves hanging out with us. He shows up for every family celebration. He referees when we bicker. He energizes us when we're exhausted. He comforts us when we don't know which way to turn. The Creator of families is present to encourage us during every step of parenting.

One mom told me, "When you start the adoption process, you don't even know what you don't even know." Adoption looks pretty easy when you're watching from the sidelines. Then, like a youngster learning to skate, you take those first tentative steps onto the ice. You fall. You haul yourself up, check for bruises, and try again, becoming more bold with each step. Suddenly you discover you're gliding…and spinning…and jumping…and crashing. But you keep training. And as you do, you discover adoption simultaneously surprises, challenges, and delights.

As you suit up for adoptive parenthood, stride onto the ice with confidence. God, your partner, is ready to balance, support, and guide you. He's reaching out for you. Will you grab His hand?

Acknowledgments

As I wrote this book I jotted down names of those whose input and encouragement helped bring it to fruition. The list grew continually, reminding me that writing is not an isolated endeavor but rather, a melding of many voices—a byproduct of the efforts of dozens.

Our journey to adoption and the impetus for this book began with our sons' birth families, notably Jen Steele and Karen and Blaine Hall. Your enthusiastic support and willingness to share some of the most difficult moments of your lives is awe-inspiring.

My three boys, Robert, Ben, and Josh, have walked every step of this journey with me. Thank you for allowing me to share our story. Robert, I especially appreciate your uncanny ability to supply precisely the right word when my numbed brain refused to cooperate, for entertaining the boys during my writing jags, and for sustaining me with hugs and decaf mochas.

Ben, you've cheerfully allowed your "writing mom" to humiliate you in front of your classmates year after year. Thanks for surprising me with homemade iced frappuccinos during my afternoon slumps.

Josh, you unfailingly asked how my writing was coming along. One day, when I'd been writing for two hours and had produced only two sentences, you inquired, "How big were the sentences?" Thank you for warning me when I was working too hard and for intuitively sensing when I most needed a hug—and giving it. I love you guys!

I'd have been lost without my most cherished writer friends, the girls from SWiG (Snohomish Writers Group), who've told me, "It's only a matter of time," since the day I began looking for a home for this project. Jenn Doucette, queen of chapter titles: thanks for your never-ending delight in talking about writing, day or night. Kari Brodin, I appreciate your professional proofreading eyes. Janet McElvaine, I love the way you thoughtfully chew on my words. Loree Cameron, I admire your attentiveness and prayerful spirit. Sheri Plucker, I'm inspired by your unique perspective on life and parenting. My Jane Austen action figure salutes you all with her quill pen.

Lisa Ebbesen and Cindy Laxton, I'm ever grateful for your invitation to join you at the International Christian Retail Show 2005, where we met the wonderful folks from Harvest House. Julie Barnhill, thank you for encouraging me to pitch my book idea to Harvest House and for praying with me before I went in to play hardball.

Steve Miller championed my book when most publishers thought that a book about adoption—particularly one from a Christian worldview—would never fly. Your calm, steady support means the world to me. Special thanks goes to my fantabulous editor (and fellow adoptive parent), Paul Gossard. I'm also grateful for the many others at Harvest House who've cheerfully offered assistance and made me feel special: Sharon Burke, Carolyn McCready, Betty Fletcher, Laura Knudson, and Pat Mathis. It's an honor to work with you.

I greatly appreciate the assistance of my fabulous indexer and librarian extraordinaire, Sue Dryer. Thank you for your labor of love on my behalf.

A special thanks to my cheerleaders: my dad, Glen Hutchison; my brother, Andrew Hutchison, whose bizarre sense of humor keeps me from taking myself too seriously; my sister-in-law, Amy Hutchison, for firsthand insights about life as "an adopted person"; my in-laws, Jim and Kay Christianson; my sister-in-law, Carole Balcells, for actively listening to me process my thoughts; my sweet nieces, Ana and Katrina Balcells, who share my passion for writing and who are my biggest little fans.

Rounding out the cheerleading squad: Mike and Patti Anderson, Rich and Sheryl Bullock, Suzanne Chandler, Jan C., Denise Easter, Lisa Johnson, Carey Kerns, Dianna Kunce, Diane Lostrangio, Aimeé Poché, Jim Rubart, Kyle and Aundi Russell, Julie Wilson, and the folks from Heartbeat Ministries at University Presbyterian Church in Seattle—I'm grateful for your encouragement, your assistance, and your advice.

Dozens of people offered insights, anecdotes, and slices of their lives as the book was birthed (or should I say, *adopted?*). Your thoughts are the heart and soul of this book. The hugest of thanks to all who participated—those named within these pages and those who preferred to remain anonymous.

Finally, but most importantly, I'm grateful to God, who provided the inspiration for the words written here. Thank You for giving me a spirit of determination and for encouraging me to be Your ambassador.

We are therefore Christ's ambassadors,
as though God were making his appeal through us.

2 Corinthians 5:20

Questions and Ideas for Reflection or Discussion

Chapter 1: We Need a Hero

1. List your primary reasons for expanding your family through adoption.

2. List reasons you feel reluctant to adopt or areas of concern you want to resolve before moving ahead with adoption.

3. On a scale of 1 to 5, rate your enthusiasm and readiness to adopt. If you're married, rate your spouse's enthusiasm. Discuss your ratings together.

4. How do you feel about being labeled "adoptive parent"? How do you feel about your child being labeled "adopted"?

5. How will you respond to those who oppose your decision to adopt?

6. Create a plan for announcing your intention to adopt to your extended family.

Chapter 2: Attached at the Heart

1. How important is it for your child to resemble you? When others comment that your child doesn't look or act like you, how will you respond?

2. Think of instances in which you have loved intentionally. How will you practice "the discipline of loving" your child?

3. List three ways you will affirm your child's uniqueness and help your child develop a sense of "belonging" in your family.

Chapter 3: Pass the Bucks

1. Request information packets from your state or province's public adoption agency and from three private adoption agencies, two adoption attorneys, and two adoption facilitators. Compare programs, fees, and services for each.

2. Create an adoption budget, estimating the fees you'll likely pay based on your research of adoption service providers.

3. Outline five steps you will take to supplement your adoption budget (list specific loans, subsidies, grants, corporate donations, and workplace benefits you plan to investigate).

4. Create an adoption fund. Set a goal for a specific amount you will add to the fund during a six-month period based on savings generated through frugal living and/or creative fundraising.

Chapter 4: Labor of Love

1. With a partner, role-play scenarios in which you tactfully respond to frequently asked questions about the adoption process.

2. List issues you believe may prevent you from being a candidate for adoption. Contact an adoption social worker and ask him or her how those issues may affect your chances of adopting.

3. Using the checklist in chapter 4, list three characteristics you would most prefer in a child, and three characteristics you would prefer to avoid.

4. Imagine you're pregnant and considering placing your child for adoption. What would you want to know about the prospective adoptive parents of your child?

5. Imagine you're writing a letter to the birth parents of the child you hope to adopt. What would you tell them about yourself?

6. List five specific ways your supporters can help you immediately after your child arrives in your home.

Chapter 5: Missed Conception

1. Discuss the following question with your partner: *Do we want to be pregnant or do we want to be parents?*

2. Have you mourned the death of your dream for a biological child? If so, how are you currently managing your infertility? If not, what steps will you take to grieve your loss and manage your infertility?

3. How will you respond to those who claim infertility is a result of unconfessed sin?

4. How has infertility impacted your spiritual journey?

5. How will you respond to those who advise, *"Adopt and you'll get pregnant"*?

6. For two weeks, test drive the "five-minute rule" with your partner.

Chapter 6: Out of Sight, Out of Mind

1. List misgivings, stereotypes, or fears you have about birth parents. Ask your adoption professional to introduce you to a person who has placed a child for adoption, and candidly discuss your misgivings with that person.

2. Put yourself in the place of a woman or man who is considering releasing a child for adoption. What concerns would you have about adoption? About the prospective adoptive parents of your child?

3. What new insights do you have about birth mothers after studying the story of Jochebed and Moses?

4. List three ways you will encourage a woman or man who is grieving after placing a child for adoption.

Chapter 7: Adoption Miscarriage

1. Have you had to share the news of a failed adoption with loved ones? How did your loved ones react? How do you wish they'd reacted?

2. If you have experienced adoption loss, have you given yourself permission to grieve?

3. As you grieve adoption loss, what brings you the greatest comfort?

4. How do you think God feels when you vent your anger over adoption loss at Him? Will you ask God to invade your grief with joy?

Chapter 8: Out-of-Diaper Experience

1. With a partner, role-play the ways you'll respond to nosy questions about your child.

2. List the pros and cons of adopting an older child versus a younger child as they pertain to your life circumstances.

3. If there are other children in your family, how will you include them when deciding whether to expand your family through adoption?

4. How will you help every child in your family adjust to the arrival of a new sibling?

5. Do you plan to change your child's name? Why or why not? What impact might a name change have on your child?

6. How do you anticipate you'll react if your child is unable to express affection towards you or to accept your love?

7. Brainstorm five ways you will help your child thrive in your family.

8. List five ways you will seek support before, during, and after adopting your child.

Chapter 9: International Intrigue

1. List the top three reasons you would adopt internationally instead of domestically.

2. How do you plan to discuss your child's birth family with him or her?

3. What risk factors are most prevalent in the country from which you're adopting (malnutrition, fetal alcohol exposure, neglect)? Create a plan to address specific risk factors.

4. Develop a database of pediatricians in your area who specialize in adoption medicine. Schedule a pre-adoption consultation.

Chapter 10: Culture Club

1. List ten ways in which your child's birth culture and daily routine differs from yours.

2. List specific ideas for helping your child process culture shock.

3. Research interpreter services in your area. Plan how you will bridge the language barrier during your child's first few months home.

4. Investigate ways to celebrate your child's ethnic and cultural heritage.

Chapter 11: Different Strokes

1. On a scale of 1 to 5, how do you rate your comfort level with becoming a transracial family?

2. As you read this chapter, did you become aware of any racial prejudices you weren't aware you had? If so, how will you work through those prejudices?

222   *The* Adoption Decision

3. List your two biggest concerns about adopting a child of a different race.

4. With a partner, rehearse how you'll respond to questions about your transracial family. Just for the fun of it, brainstorm at least one humorous response.

5. Brainstorm age-appropriate ways in which you will acquaint your child with racism.

6. Strategize responses to racist jokes, dirty looks, insults, and inferior treatment directed at either your family or your child.

7. List three practical ways you will facilitate "color awareness" and help your child develop a healthy racial and ethnic identity.

Chapter 12: Love Me Tender, Love Me Sweet

1. If your adoption social worker asked you to consider adopting a child with medical challenges, how would you respond?

2. List the medical challenges you feel best equipped to handle. List those you feel least equipped to handle. In what ways are you willing to adjust your life to accommodate your child's needs?

3. If you already have children and are considering adopting a child with medical challenges, how do you anticipate your family dynamic will change?

4. Reread the suggestions on pages 170–171 for how to assemble a support system. Pencil in dates on your calendar for each item on the checklist.

5. List three concrete ways you will reach out to a family who has a child with medical challenges.

Chapter 13: My DNA Made Me Do It

1. Research several of the most common challenges adopted children face: learning differences, Attention Deficit Disorder, attachment problems, Post-Traumatic Stress Disorder, depres-

sion, and other mental health issues. What services are available in your area should your child experience one or more of these challenges?

2. Talk to a person whose child has behavioral challenges. Ask the person to candidly explain the ups and downs of parenting a child with challenges.

3. Learn about the accommodations available for behaviorally-challenged children at local day-care facilities, public and private schools, and at your church.

4. Meet with leaders in your church to brainstorm ways your faith community can support special-needs families.

Chapter 14: Open-Door Policy

1. On a scale of 1 to 5, how comfortable do you feel about interacting with your child's birth family before the adoption? After the adoption?

2. Which of the four concerns regarding openness applies most to you? List two steps you will take to conquer your primary fear.

3. Brainstorm five ways you will set healthy boundaries around the relationship between you and your child's birth family. Discuss your ideas with your adoption social worker. If possible, discuss them with your child's birth family.

4. *Truthfulness* and *trust* are the hallmarks of open adoption. List specific ways you will nurture those qualities within relationships formed through adoption.

Chapter 15: ...For the Bible Tells Me So

1. List three similarities between first century and twenty-first century adoption practices.

2. Explain how the Roman adoption concept of being "born again" parallels spiritual rebirth.

3. How does knowing that Jesus is praying on your behalf impact you as you prepare for adoptive parenthood?

4. List three practical ways you will extend *agape* love to your child.

5. If you have not already done so, consider inviting God to partner with you during your journey through adoption.

Recommended Resources

Books

Memoirs and First-Person Reflections

Beazely, Jan. *The Strength of Mercy.* Colorado Springs, CO: Water-Brook Press, 1999.

Doxon, Lynn Ellen. *Rainbows from Heaven: A Story of Faith, Hope and Love that Created a Family.* Rocky Mount, NC: Artemesia Publishing, 2004.

Gardner, Michelle. *Adoption as a Ministry, Adoption as a Blessing.* Enumclaw, WA: WinePress Publishing, 2003.

———. *After the Dream Comes True: Post-Adoption Support for Christian Families* (Enumclaw, WA: WinePress Publishing, 2004.

Hannah, Deborah L. *An Unlit Path: One Family's Journey Toward the Light of Truth.* Fairfax, VA: Xulon Press, 2006.

John, Jaiya. *Black Baby White Hands: A View from the Crib.* Silver Spring, MD: Soul Water Rising, 2005.

Laskas, Jeanne Marie. *Growing Girls: The Mother of All Adventures.* New York, NY: Bantam Dell, 2006.

Page, Katheryn J. *Returned with Love: A Story of the Pain and Joy of Adoption.* Enumclaw, WA: WinePress Publishing, 2005.

Register, Cheri. *Beyond Good Intentions: A Mother Reflects on Raising Internationally Adopted Children.* St. Paul, MN: Yeong and Yeong Book Company, 2005.

Reid, Theresa. *Two Little Girls: A Memoir of Adoption.* New York, NY: The Berkley Publishing Group, 2006.

Tucker, Neely. *Love in the Driest Season: A Family Memoir.* New York, NY: Crown Publishers, 2004.

Wolff, Jana. *Secret Thoughts of an Adoptive Mother.* Honolulu, HI: Vista Communications, 2000.

Wong, Kristin Swick. *Carried Safely Home: The Spiritual Legacy of an Adoptive Family.* Grand Haven, MI: FaithWalk Publishing, 2005.

Support and Guidance

Allender, Dan B., and Larry Crabb. *Hope When You're Hurting: Answers to Four Questions Hurting People Ask.* Grand Rapids, MI: Zondervan, 1997.

Babb, L. Anne, and Rita Laws. *Adopting and Advocating for the Special Needs Child: A Guide for Parents and Professionals.* Westport, CT: Bergin and Garvey, 1997.

Caldwell, Mardie. *AdoptingOnline.com.* Nevada City, CA: American Carriage House Publishing, 2004.

———. *Adoption: Your Step-by-Step Guide.* Nevada City, CA: American Carriage House Publishing, 2005.

Christianson, Laura. *The Adoption Network: Your Guide to Starting a Support System.* Enumclaw, WA: WinePress Publishing Group, 2007.

Coughlin, Amy, and Caryn Abramowitz. *Cross-Cultural Adoption: How to Answer Questions from Family, Friends, and Community.* Washington, DC: Lifeline Press, 2004.

Crawford, Mark E. *When Two Become Three: Nurturing Your Marriage After Baby Arrives.* Grand Rapids, MI: Revell, 2007.

Davenport, Dawn. *The Complete Book of International Adoption: A Step-by-Step Guide to Finding Your Child.* New York: Broadway Books, 2006.

Dormon, Sara, and Ruth Graham. *So You Want to Adopt...Now What?: A Practical Guide for Navigating the Adoption Process.* Ventura, CA: Regal Books, 2006.

Eldridge, Sherri. *Twenty Life-Transforming Choices Adoptees Need to Make.* Colorado Springs, CO: Piñon Press, 2003.

———. *Twenty Things Adopted Kids Wish Their Adoptive Parents Knew.* Delta, 1999.

Evans, Karin. *The Lost Daughters of China: Abandoned Girls, Their Journey to America, and the Search for a Missing Past.* New York, NY: Tarcher, 2001.

Felder, Leonard. *When Difficult Relatives Happen to Good People.* Emmaus, PA: Rodale Press, 2003; difficultrelatives.com.

Foli, Karen J., and John R. Thompson. *The Post-Adoption Blues: Overcoming the Unforseen Challenges of Adoption.* Emmaus, PA: Rodale Books, 2004.

Gillespie, Natalie Nichols. *Successful Adoption: A Guide for Christian Families.* Franklin, TN: Integrity Publishers, 2006.

Goodwin, Debbie Salter. *Empowering Your Child Who Has Special Needs.* Kansas City, MO: Beacon Hill Press of Kansas City, 2006.

Gray, Deborah D. *Attaching in Adoption: Practical Tools for Today's Parents.* Indianapolis, IN: Perspectives Press, 2002.

Harrison, Nick, and Steve Miller. *The Best-Ever Christian Baby Name Book.* Eugene, OR: Harvest House Publishers, 2007.

Hopkins-Best, Mary. *Toddler Adoption: The Weaver's Craft.* Indianapolis, IN: Perspectives Press, 1998.

Hunter, Laura, and Jennifer Walker. *The Moms on Call Guide to Basic Baby Care: The First Six Months*. Grand Rapids, MI: Revell, 2007.

Johnston, Patricia Irwin. *Adopting After Infertility*. Indianapolis, IN: Perspectives Press, 1992.

Keck, Gregory C., and Regina Kupecky. *Adopting the Hurt Child: Hope for Families with Special Needs Kids*. Colorado Springs, CO: NavPress, 1998.

———. *Parenting the Hurt Child: Helping Adoptive Families Heal and Grow*. Colorado Springs, CO: Piñon Press, 2002.

Keefer, Betsy, and Jayne E. Schooler. *Telling the Truth to Your Adopted or Foster Child: Making Sense of the Past*. Westport, CT: Bergin & Garvey Trade, 2000.

Leman, Kevin. *Single Parenting That Works*. Carol Stream, IL: Tyndale House Publishers, 2006.

London, Nancy. *Hot Flashes, Warm Bottles*. Berkeley, CA: Celestial Arts, 2001.

Martin, Cynthia D., and Dru Martin Groves. *Beating the Adoption Odds: Using Your Head and Your Heart to Adopt*. Orlando, FL: Harcourt Brace & Company, 1998.

Maskew, Trish. *Our Own: Adopting and Parenting the Older Child*. Longmont, CO: Snowcap Press, 1999.

Melina, Lois Ruskai, *Raising Adopted Children*. New York: Harper-Perennial, 1998.

Melina, Lois Ruskai and Sharon Kaplan Roszia. *The Open Adoption Experience*. New York, NY: HarperPerennial, 1993.

Melosh, Barbara. *Strangers and Kin: The American Way of Adoption*. Cambridge, MA: Harvard University Press, 2002.

Miller, Laurie C. *The Handbook of International Adoption Medicine: A Guide for Physicians, Parents, and Providers*. Oxford: Oxford University Press, 2004.

Mintzer, Richard. *Yes, You Can Adopt*. New York: Carroll & Graf Publishers, 2003.

Pertman, Adam. *Adoption Nation: How the Adoption Revolution Is Transforming America.* New York: Basic Books, 2001.

Smith, Gordon T. *Listening to God in Times of Choice: The Art of Discerning God's Will.* Downers Grove, IL: InterVarsity Press, 1997.

Stevenson-Moessner, Jeanne. *The Spirit of Adoption: At Home in God's Family.* Louisville, KY: Westminster John Knox Press, 2003.

Varon, Lee. *Adopting on Your Own: The Complete Guide to Adopting as a Single Parent.* New York: Farrar, Straus and Giroux, 2000.

Voght, Beth K. *Baby Changes Everything: Embracing and Preparing for Motherhood after 35.* Grand Rapids, MI: Revell, 2007.

Wright, Marguerite A. *I'm Chocolate, You're Vanilla: Raising Healthy Black and Biracial Children in a Race-Conscious World.* Hoboken, NJ: Jossey-Bass, 2000.

Anthologies

Holloway, Sara, ed. *Family Wanted: Stories of Adoption.* New York: Random House, 2005.

Kingsbury, Karen. *A Treasury of Adoption Miracles: True Stories of God's Presence Today.* New York: Warner Faith, 2005.

Klatzkin, Amy. *A Passage to the Heart: Writings from Families with Children from China.* St. Paul, MN: Yeong and Yeong Book Company, 1999.

Krebs, Betsy, and Paul Pitcoff. *Beyond the Foster Care System: The Future for Teens.* New Brunswick, NJ: Rutgers University Press, 2006.

Kruger, Pamela, and Jill Smolowe, eds. *A Love Like No Other: Stories from Adoptive Parents.* New York: Riverhead Books, 2005.

Trenka, Jane Jeong, et al., eds., *Outsiders Within: Writing on Transracial Adoption.* Cambridge, MA: South End Press, 2006.

Wegar, Katarina, ed. *Adoptive Families in a Diverse Society.* New Brunswick, NJ: Rutgers University Press, 2006.

Adoption-Related Fiction

Bentz, Joseph. *Cradle of Dreams*. Bloomington, MN: Bethany House Publishers, 2001.

Bradford, Joanna McGee. *The Father's Voice*. Chicago: Moody Publishers, 2006.

Buckman, Michelle. *A Piece of the Sky*. Colorado Springs, CO: River Oak, 2005.

Dobson, Melanie. *Together for Good*. Grand Rapids, MI: Kregel Publications, 2006.

Gould, Leslie. *Beyond the Blue*. Colorado Springs, CO: WaterBrook Press, 2005.

————. *Scrap Everything*. Colorado Springs, CO: WaterBrook Press, 2006.

Kingsbury, Karen. *Like Dandelion Dust*. Nashville, TN: Center Street, 2006.

————. *Oceans Apart*. Grand Rapids, MI: Zondervan, 2004.

Lasinski, Kirsten. *Guarded*. Chicago: Moody Publishers, 2005.

Tyler, Anne. *Digging to America*. New York: Alfred A. Knopf, 2006.

VanLiere, Donna. *The Christmas Hope*. Franklin, TN: Integrity Publishers, 2005.

Unplanned Pregnancy

Dormon, Sara, and Ruth Graham. *I'm Pregnant...Now What?: Heartfelt Advice on Getting Through an Unplanned Pregnancy*. Ventura, CA: Regal Books, 2004.

Fieker, Sharon. *I Choose This Day: Mournings and Miracles of Adoption*. Mustang, OK: Tate Publishing, 2006.

Schooler, Jayne E., *Mom, Dad, I'm Pregnant: When Your Daughter or Son Faces an Unplanned Pregnancy*. Colorado Springs, CO: NavPress, 2004.

Infertility Books

Canady, Ty. *What to Expect When You're Not Expecting.* Lincoln, NE: iUniverse, 2003.

Forbus, Beth. *Baby Hunger: Biblical Encouragement for Those Struggling with Infertility.* Fairfax, VA: Xulon Press, 2003.

Gibbs, Donna, et al. *Water from the Rock: Finding God's Comfort in the Midst of Infertility.* Chicago: Moody Publishers, 2002.

Glahn, Sandra L., and William R. Cutrer. *When Empty Arms Become a Heavy Burden: Encouragement for Couples Facing Infertility.* Nashville, TN: Broadman & Holman Publishers, 1996.

———. *The Infertility Companion: Hope and Help for Couples Facing Infertility.* Grand Rapids, MI: Zondervan, 2004.

Peoples, Debby, and Harriette Rovner Ferguson. *Experiencing Infertility.* New York: W.W. Norton & Company, 1998.

Schalesky, Marlo. *Empty Womb, Aching Heart: Hope and Help for Those Struggling with Infertility.* Bloomington, MN: Bethany House Publishers, 2001.

Skaradzinski, Anne and Daryl. *We're in This Together: Our Story of Infertility and Love.* Milwaukee, WI: 416 Publishing, 2006.

Woodward, Shannon. *Inconceivable: Finding Peace in the Midst of Infertility.* Colorado Springs, CO: Life Journey, 2006.

Devotionals

Fuller, Nina. *Special Strength for Special Parents: 31 Days of Spiritual Therapy for Parents of Special Needs Children.* Evansville, IN: GMA Publishing, 2006.

Garrett, Ginger. *Moments for Couples Who Long for Children.* Colorado Springs, CO: NavPress, 2003.

Saake, Jennifer. *Hannah's Hope: Seeking God's Heart in the Midst of Infertility, Miscarriage and Adoption Loss.* Colorado Springs, CO: NavPress, 2005.

Wunnenberg, Kathe. *Longing for a Child: Devotions of Hope for Your Journey Through Infertility.* Grand Rapids, MI: Zondervan, 2005.

————. *Grieving the Child I Never Knew.* Grand Rapids, MI: Zondervan, 2001.

Magazines and Periodicals

Adoption

Adoption TODAY (adoptinfo.net). 541 E. Garden Dr., Unit N, Windsor, CO 80550.

Adoptive Families (adoptivefamilies.com). 39 West 37th Street, 15th Floor, New York, NY 10018. 646-366-0830.

Fostering Families TODAY (fosteringfamiliestoday.com). 541 E. Garden Dr., Unit N, Windsor, CO 80550.

Infertility

Achieving Families (achievingfamilies.com). P.O. Box 99, Barrington, IL 60011.

Conceive Magazine (conceiveonline.com). 622 East Washington Street, Suite 440, Orlando, FL 32801. 800-758-0770.

Stepping Stones (bethany.org/step). C/o Bethany Christian Services, 901 Eastern Avenue NE, P.O. Box 294, Grand Rapids, MI 49501-0294. 616-224-7488.

Online Resources

Adopt America Network. (AdoptAmericaNetwork.org)—National nonprofit organization that matches special needs children to adoptive parents. Emphasis is placed on children who have been abused, neglected; have medical, physical and/or emotional challenges; are of minority heritage; have siblings, or are school age or older.

Adopting.com. Directory of adoption resources, including agencies, support groups, and photo listings.

Adoption.com. Information for all members of the adoption triad; weekly e-newsletter, blog network; discussion forums; photo listing of U.S. and international waiting children; profiles of hopeful families.

AdoptUsKids.org. Largest national photo listing from the Children's Bureau, part of the Federal Department of Health and Human Services.

American Academy of Adoption Attorneys. (AdoptionAttorneys .org). National association of attorneys who practice adoption law.

American Academy of Pediatrics Section on Adoption and Foster Care (aap.org/sections/adoption/). Nearly 200 medical professionals nationwide who provide care to and/or research health issues related to foster care and/or adoption.

Association for Treatment and Training in the Attachment of Children (ATTACh) (attach.org). Up-to-date information about attachment issues and treatment options for parents and professionals. Includes a directory of qualified treatment professionals.

BirthMom Buds (birthmombuds.com). A peeer-support network of over 400 women worldwide who are considering adoption or who have placed children for adoption.

Child Welfare Information Gateway (childwelfare.gov/). Publications, statistics, and state statutes on all aspects of domestic and intercountry adoption.

ComeUnity (comeunity.com/). Articles, resources, and support for adoptive parents and for those parenting children with special needs.

Evan B. Donaldson Adoption Institute (AdoptionInstitute.org). Research about adoption law, policies, and practices.

FamilyLife's Hope for Orphans (familylife.com/hopefororphans/). Ministry dedicated to connecting orphaned children with Christian adoptive families.

Hannah's Prayer Ministries (hannahsprayer.org). Christian support for fertility challenges, including primary and secondary infertility, pregnancy loss, early infant death, and adoption loss.

iParenting.com. A network of parenting sites, including adoption, fertility, and special kids.

Karen's Adoption Links (karensadoptionlinks.com). Links to organizations, statistics, listservs, financing information, parenting resources, multicultural products, and more.

National Adoption Center (adopt.org/). Photo listing of U.S. waiting children; resource library, chats; e-zine.

RainbowKids.com. Helps for those planning intercountry adoption.

Suite 101: Special Needs Parenting (specialneedsparenting. suite101.com/). Articles for parents whose children face challenges such as autism, ADHD, hearing or visual impairments, and Down syndrome.

Tapestry Books (tapestrybooks.com). Online bookstore specializing in the sale of adoption books.

Yahoo Groups (groups.yahoo.com). Discussion groups centered around all types and aspects of adoption.

Online Resources for Financing Adoption

Adoption-Friendly Workplace Program (AdoptionFriendlyWorkplace.org), 877-777-4222. Free materials to help people advocate for adoption benefits in their workplace.

Adoption Subsidy Resource Center (nacac.org/adoptionsubsidy .html), 800-470-6665. Profiles state and Canadian province adoption subsidy programs available for children with special needs.

AffordingAdoption.com. Links to grants, loans, employer benefits, and tips for fundraising and saving money on adoption travel.

Dave Thomas Foundation For Adoption, (www.davethomasfoun dationforadoption.org), 800-275-3832. Nonprofit organization dedicated to increasing the adoptions of children in North America's foster care systems.

The Family and Medical Leave Act (dol.gov/esa/whd/fmla/). Requires employers with 50 or more employees to offer eligible employees up to 12 weeks of unpaid leave upon the birth or adoption of a child.

Federal Adoption Tax Credit (irs.gov/taxtopics/tc607.html; irs.gov/publications/p968/index.html), Publication 968. Explains the details of the tax credit available to eligible families.

The Foundation Directory (fconline.fdncenter.org/). All-inclusive foundation data, available for subscription online or in the reference section of public libraries.

Frugal Adoptions (groups.yahoo.com/group/FRUGAL_ADOPTIONS). E-mail discussion group for people who live frugally in order to fund their adoptions and ongoing household expenses.

Gift of Adoption Fund (GiftOfAdoption.org). Awards one-time grants to assist parents who are in the final stages of adoption financing.

National Endowment for Financial Education (www.nefe.org/adoption/), 303-741-6333. Helpful information about how to make adoption an affordable option.

National Military Family Association (nmfa.org/site/DocServer/DoD_Adoption_Reimbursement_3-10-06.pdf?docID=5301). Fact sheet about the DoD Adoption Reimbursement Program, which reimburses active-duty personnel for most one-time adoption costs up to $2000 per child, with a maximum reimbursement to one service member of $5000 in any calendar year.

Shaohannah's Hope Foundation (shaohannahshope.org). Awards grants to qualified Christian families who are in the process of adopting.

Notes

Chapter 1—We Need a Hero

1. The Dave Thomas Foundation for Adoption and The Evan B. Donaldson Adoption Institute, *National Adoption Attitudes Survey,* June 2002, p. 2; *Adoptive Families* magazine media kit; Adam Pertman, *Adoption Nation* (Basic Books: Boulder, CO: 2001), p. 29, quoting: J.H. Hollinger, "Aftermath of Adoption: Legal and Social Consequences," *Adoption Law and Practice,* pp. 13/1-13/113.

2. See James 1:27; Psalm 82:3-4.

3. The Dave Thomas Foundation, p. 1.

4. U.S. Department of Agriculture, Center for Nutrition Policy and Promotion, "Expenditures on Children by Families, 2005" (Miscellaneous Publication Number 1528-2005, www.usda.gov/cnpp/Crc/crc2005.pdffinancial security), p. 12.

5. Jill Smolowe, "The Reluctant Spouse," *Adoptive Families,* September/October 1998, reprinted July/August 2000. Also available at www.babycenter.com/essay/preconception/adopting/1374888.html.

6. See, respectively, Romans 8:26; Ephesians 3:16-19 MSG.

7. Margaret Olander, "Announcing Your Decision to Adopt," *Adoptive Families,* March/April 2003, pp. 19-20.

8. Exodus 14:14.

Chapter 2—Attached at the Heart

1. See Matthew 19:5-6.

2. 1 Peter 1:4; see Romans 3:23-25.

3. Luke 22:18-20 MSG.

4. 1 Corinthians 10:16-17 MSG.

5. Rita Laws, *Adopting and Advocating for the Special Needs Child* (Westport, CT: Bergin & Garvey, 1997), p. 23.

6. See 1 Peter 1:13,17,22.

7. 1 John 3:1; see 1 John 3:18.

8. Jana Wolff, "You Have to be Perfect to Adopt…And Other Myths," *Adoptive Families*, www.adoptivefamilies.com/articles .php?aid=169.

9. Psalm 139:13-16 MSG.

Chapter 3—Pass the Bucks

1. The Dave Thomas Foundation for Adoption and The Evan B. Donaldson Adoption Institute, *National Adoption Attitudes Survey,* June 2002, p. 9; "National Profile of Adoptive Families," *U.S. Department of Commerce News,* Washington, DC, August 22, 2003 (also: Census 2000, U.S. Census Bureau).

2. U.S. Department of Labor, U.S. Bureau of Labor Statistics, *National Compensation Survey: Employee Benefits in Private Industry in the United States,* March 2006, August 2006 (www .bls.gov/ncs/ebs/sp/ebsm0004.pdf), p. 28 (see also, *Working Mother,* October 2006, p. 74; *Adoptive Families,* October 2005, p. 12.; *USA Today* Information Network (www.adoptioninsti tute.org/quiz/quizint.html), August 25, 1997.

3. Adoption Friendly Workplace (www.AdoptionFriendlyWork place.org), 1-877-777-4222.

4. Internal Revenue Service, "Tax Law Changes for Individuals: Adoption Credit and Adoption Assistance Programs" (www.irs.gov/formspubs/article/0,,id=109876,00 .html#exempt_2006).

5. See Psalm 127:3 MSG; 1 Chronicles 28–29.

6. 1 Chronicles 28:20.

7. Psalm 116:16 MSG.

Chapter 4—Labor of Love

1. Grace Fox, *10-Minute Time-Outs for Moms* (Eugene, OR: Harvest House, 2004), p. 166.

2. Jill Smolowe, *An Empty Lap: One Couple's Journey to Parenthood* (New York: Pocket Books, 1998), p. 167.

3. Theresa Reid, *Two Little Girls: A Memoir of Adoption* (New York: The Berkley Publishing Group, 2006), p. 15.

4. Kristin Swick Wong, *Carried Safely Home: The Spiritual Legacy of an Adoptive Family* (Grand Haven, MI: Faithwalk Publishing, 2005), p. 9.

5. 1 Thessalonians 5:16-18 MSG and Romans 12:12 MSG.

6. See James 1:5; 4:8; Psalm 119:105; 18:36.

Chapter 5—Missed Conception

1. Job 2:11 MSG.

2. Job 4:7;11:14,16,18 MSG.

3. Job 7:11 MSG.

4. Job 42:1 MSG.

5. Larry Crabb and Dan B. Allender, *Hope When You're Hurting: Answers to Four Questions Hurting People Ask* (Grand Rapids, MI: Zondervan, 1997), p. 173.

6. See Job 23:11.

7. 1 Peter 5:7.

8. See 1 Samuel 1:1-20.

9. Helmut Thielicke, transl. J. W. Doberstein, *Christ and the Meaning of Life—Sermons* (New York: Harper & Brothers, 1962), pp. 18-19.

10. Matthew 11:28 MSG.

11. See Revelation 21:4; Psalm 30:11 MSG; Isaiah 51:11.

12. Debby Peoples and Harriette Rovner Ferguson, *Experiencing Infertility* (New York: WW Norton & Company), p. 31.

Chapter 6—Out of Sight, Out of Mind

1. Child Welfare Information Gateway, "Voluntary Relinquishment for Adoption: Numbers and Trends" (www.childwelfare.gov/pubs/s_place.cfm), 2005; S.M. Bianchi, "America's Children: Mixed Prospects," *Population Bulletin* (June 1990), p. 45, 1:9-10.

2. Mary Ruth Colby, "Protection of Children in Adoption," National Conference of Social Work, June 28, 1938, Central File 1937-1940. Estimate for 1945 cited in E. Wayne Carp, *Family Matters: Secrecy and Disclosure in the History of Adoption* (Cambridge: Harvard University Press), 1998, p. 29.

3. Gordon Scott Bonham, "Who Adopts: The Relationship of Adoption and Social-Demographic Characteristics of Women," *Journal of Marriage and the Family* (National Center for Health Statistics), May 1977, pp. 295-306; C.A. Bachrach et al., "Relinquishment of Premarital Births: Evidence from National Survey Data," *Family Planning Perspectives,* Jan/Feb 1992, p. 24.

4. U.S. Bureau of the Census, "Households by Type: 1940 to Present," www.census.gov/population/socdemo/hh-fam/tabHH-1.pdf, Table HH-1, September 15, 2004.

5. National Center for Health Statistics, "Births to Teenagers in the United States, 1940–2000," vol. 49, no. 10, September 25, 2001, pp. 2, 4, 10.

6. Bachrach, et al., pp. 24, 27-32, 48.

7. Cynthia Dailard, "Reviving Interest in Policies and Programs to Help Teens Prevent Repeat Births," *The Guttmacher Report on Public Policy,* vol. 3, no. 3, June 2000.

8. Used by permission.

9. Exodus 1:22 MSG.

Chapter 7—Adoption Miscarriage

1. Adam Pertman, *Adoption Nation: How the Adoption Revolution Is Transforming America* (New York: Basic Books, 2000), p. 10.

2. Child Welfare Information Gateway, "Consent to Adoption: Summary of State Laws," State Statutes Series, 2004 (www .childwelfare.gov/systemwide/laws_policies/statutes/consen tall.pdf).

3. R.M. Goerge et al., S., *Adoption, Disruption, and Displacement in the Child Welfare System, 1976-94* (Chicago: University of Chicago, Chapin Hall Center for Children,1994). Also: Child Welfare Information Gateway, "Adoption Disruption and Dissolution: Numbers and Trends," 2004 (www.childwelfare.gov/pubs/s_disrup.cfm).

4. Child Welfare Information Gateway, "Adoption Disruption and Dissolution."

5. Child Welfare Information Gateway, "Adoption Disruption and Dissolution."

6. Barbara Johnson, *Splashes of Joy in the Cesspools of Life* (Nashville, TN: W Publishing Group, 1992), pp. 39-40.

7. Johnson, p. 40.

8. See Luke 6:37; Mark 11:25; Matthew 6:14-15; also, Luke 11:4.

9. Isaiah 43:1-4 MSG.

10. Dietrich Bonhoeffer, *Life Together: A Discussion of Christian Fellowship* (San Francisco: Harper & Row, 1954), p. 97.

11. Bonhoeffer, pp. 98-99.

12. 2 Corinthians 12:9.

13. See Isaiah 49:16; Jeremiah 31:13 MSG.

Chapter 8—Out-of-Diaper Experience

1. U.S. Department of State, Bureau of Consular Affairs, "Immigrant Visas Issues to Orphans Coming to the U.S." Fiscal year 2006 (travel.state.gov/family/adoption/stats/stats_451.html); U.S. Department of Health & Human Services, Administra tion for Children & Families, "The AFCARS Report" (www.acf.hhs.gov/programs/cb/stats_research/afcars/tar/report10 .htm).

2. Trish Maskew, *Our Own: Adopting and Parenting the Older Child* (Longmont, CO: Snowcap Press, 1999), pp. 82, 83.

3. Maskew, p. 85.

4. Jeanne Marie Laskas, *Growing Girls: The Mother of All Adventures* (New York: Bantam Dell, 2006), p. 43.

5. Sandra Fortier, "What's the Harm? Changing a Child's First Name Upon Adoption," *Fostering Families TODAY,* March/April 2006, p. 52.

6. Fortier, p. 53, referring to Vera Fahlberg, *A Child's Journey Through Placement* (Indianapolis, IN: Perspectives Press, 1994).

7. See Genesis 17:5.

8. See Genesis 35:10.

9. See John 1:42.

10. See Revelation 2:17.

11. Rita Laws, "Advocating for the Insecurely Attached Child," *Fostering Families TODAY,* Jan/Feb 2006, p. 35.

12. Nancy London, *Hot Flashes, Warm Bottles* (Berkeley, CA: Celestial Arts, 2001), p. 42.

13. Grace Fox, *10-Minute Time-Outs for Moms* (Eugene, OR: Harvest House, 2004), p. 167.

Chapter 9—International Intrigue

1. U.S. Department of State, "Immigrant Visas Issued to Orphans Coming to the U.S., Fiscal year 2006 (travel.state.gov/family/adoption/stats/stats_451.html).

2. Dave Thomas Foundation for Adoption, "A Child Is Waiting: A Beginner's Guide to Adoption" (www.davethomasfoundationforadoption.org), p. 8.

3. Trish Maskew, *Our Own: Adopting and Parenting the Older Child* (Longmont, CO: Snowcap Press, 1999), p. 155.

4. Cheri Register, *Beyond Good Intentions: A Mother Reflects on Raising Internationally Adopted Children* (St. Paul, MN: Yeong and Yeong Book Company, 2005), pp. 18-19.

5. Lois Ruskai Melina, *Raising Adopted Children* (New York: HarperPerennial 1998), p. 240.

6. Deborah Borchers, "Post-Adoption Check-Ups," *Adoptive Families,* July/August 2003, pp. 57-58.

7. *PBS Religion & Ethics Newsweekly,* "Profile: Frederick Buechner," episode no. 936, May 5, 2006 (www.pbs.org/wnet/religionandethics/week936/profile.html).

8. Scott Church, "My Beautiful Orchid" (Seattle, WA: Sabalo Images, www.scottchurchimages.com/enviro/docs/orchid.asp).

9. 1 Corinthians 13:5-8 MSG.

Chapter 11—Different Strokes

1. 1 John 2:16; 4:8,20-21 MSG.

2. See Ephesians 4:23.

3. Adam Pertman, *Adoption Nation: How the Adoption Revolution Is Transforming America* (Jackson, TN: Basic Books, 2001), p. 58.

4. 1 Peter 3:9.

5. Jaiya John, *Black Baby White Hands: A View from the Crib* (Silver Spring, MD: Soul Water Rising, 2005), pp. 50, 146, 147.

6. John, p. 35.

7. Romans 8:27,16.

Chapter 12—Love Me Tender, Love Me Sweet

1. Lee Tobin McClain, "That Special Someone," *Adoptive Families,* Jan/Feb 2005, p. 35.

2. Michelle Gardner, *Adoption as a Ministry, Adoption as a Blessing* (Enumclaw, WA: WinePress Publishing, 2003), p. 59.

3. Matthew 25:40.

4. Gardner, p. 67.

5. Debbie Salter Goodwin, *Empowering Your Child Who Has Special Needs* (Kansas City, MO: Beacon Hill Press of Kansas City, 2006), pp. 16, 18.

6. Goodwin, p. 66.

7. References for the story of Saul, David, and Mephibosheth: 1 Samuel 17; 20:15-16; see 31:1-6; see 2 Samuel 4:4; 9:7; 9:8 MSG; 9:11.

8. Psalm 27:4.

9. Goodwin, p. 11; 1 Samuel 16:7.

Chapter 13—My DNA Made Me Do It

1. Annie Stuart, "Identifying Learning Problems in Adopted Children," SchwabLearning.org (www.schwablearning.org/articles.asp?r=689).

2. Bonnie Kerker and Martha Dore, "Mental Health Needs and Treatment of Foster Youth: Barriers and Opportunities," *American Journal of Orthopsychiatry*, vol. 76, issue 1.

3. "Attachment Explained," Evergreen Psychotherapy Center, Attachment Treatment Training Center (www.attachmentexperts.com/whatisattachment.html).

4. E. James Anthony, in the foreword to *The Psychology of Adoption*, David M. Brodzinsky and Marshall D. Schechter, eds., (Oxford: Oxford University Press, 1990), p. 3.

5. Gregory Keck and Regina Kupecky, *Parenting the Hurt Child: Helping Adoptive Families Heal and Grow* (Colorado Springs, CO: Piñon Press, 2002), p. 155.

6. Keck and Kupecky, p. 33.

7. Heather Boonstra and Elizabeth Nash, "Minors and the Right to Consent to Health Care," *The Guttmacher Report on Public Policy*, August 2000, vol. 3, no. 4 (www.guttmacher.org/pubs/tgr/03/4/gr030404.html).

8. Matthew 18:5.

9. Debbie Salter Goodwin, *Empowering Your Child Who Has Special Needs* (Kansas City, MO: Beacon Hill Press of Kansas City, 2006), p. 137.

10. Goodwin, p. 136.

11. 1 Thessalonians 1:2-5 MSG.

Chapter 14—Open-Door Policy

1. Compilation from several sources, including *Adoption Quarterly* survey of agencies in 1999.

2. Adoption.com, "Adoption Gone Awry" (library.adoption.com/adoption-risks/adoption-gone-awry/article/2579/1.html).

3. Betsy Keefer and Jayne Schooler, *Telling the Truth to Your Adopted or Foster Child: Making Sense of the Past* (Westport, CT: Bergin & Garvey Trade, 2000), p. 60.

4. Keefer and Schooler, p. 16.

5. Romans 12:17.

6. Proverbs 3:5-6 MSG.

Chapter 15—...For the Bible Tells Me So

1. Genesis 1:28 MSG.

2. Genesis 15:4; 17:3-16.

3. Matthew 1:18-22.

4. William Barclay, *The Letter to the Romans* (Philadelphia: The Westminster Press, 1955), p. 110.

5. Barclay, p. 11.

6. John 3:16.

7. Ephesians 1:4-6 NRSV.

8. 1 John 3:1.

9. Hebrews 13:5 MSG; see 7:24-25 MSG.

10. Matthew 12:50 MSG.

11. Matthew 6:33.

12. Romans 8:38-39 MSG.

13. John 19:25-27.

Index

About the Author

Laura Christianson shares her passion for adoption with a worldwide audience through her award-winning "Exploring Adoption" blog. An adoptive mom, Laura founded Heartbeat Ministries, a Christian support network for adoptive families. She is a popular speaker at adoption events and writers' conferences. Laura lives in Snohomish, Washington with her husband, Robert, and their two sons.

To contact Laura or to visit the "Exploring Adoption" blog, go to www.laurachristianson.com.

■ ■ ■

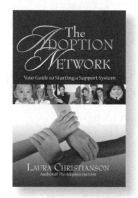

A new, helpful resource now available at Amazon.com or by contacting the author

The Adoption Network
by Laura Christianson

Do you desire to start a support network for those in your church and community whose lives are impacted by adoption?

In *The Adoption Network,* Laura Christianson, founder and director of Seattle-based Heartbeat Ministries, walks you through the basics of planning and launching a support system for adoptive families, foster families, birth parents, or adoptees. You'll learn how to:

• develop a mission statement
• plan a budget
• recruit leadership
• reach out to the community
• create workshops, support groups, social events, mentoring programs, and more

Packed with practical pointers and worksheets, this handbook will equip you with the tools you need to create a vibrant adoption support network.

ISBN-13: 978-1-57921-902-4
ISBN-10: 1-57921-902-0

helpful...fun...God-honoring...meaningful...inspiring

The Best-Ever Christian Baby Name Book
by Nick Harrison and Steve Miller

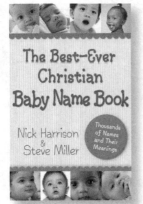

The first gift you give your child is a name. It's also the most enduring gift you'll ever give—a lifelong present that conveys meaning, a sense of identity, and often carries forward family connections and traditions.

To help you in this important and wonderful task, *The Best-Ever Christian Baby Name Book* provides a book full of great choices for your boy or girl. From Aaron to Zuwena, with lots of great variety in between, you'll discover...

- the origins and meanings of a wide selection of names

- ideas for creating a unique name especially suited for your child

- the greatest Bible names from which to choose

- what *not* to do when choosing a name

- alternate spellings and variations of your favorite names

Plus, you'll find sidebars offering additional insights into "what's in a name," as well as in-a-nutshell biographies of notable Christians with names you might like. And what else might you find in this valuable resource for one of your most important decisions as a parent? Well... you name it!

ISBN-13: 978-0-7369-1994-4
ISBN-10: 0-7369-1994-5

*To see an excerpt from this and other great books for parents, visit **www.harvesthousepublishers.com***

Helpful parenting resources
from Harvest House Publishers

365 THINGS EVERY NEW MOM SHOULD KNOW
A Daily Guide to Loving and Nurturing Your Child

Linda Danis

ISBN: 978-0-7369-0923-5

This daily guide to the first year of motherhood gives you prayerful, playful, and practical information to energize you in your new role. Features weekly devotionals and daily activities that help you foster your baby's physical, emotional, social, and spiritual growth.

THE POWER OF A PRAYING® PARENT
Stormie Omartian

ISBN: 978-0-7369-1925-8

After decades of raising her children along with her husband, Michael, bestselling author Stormie Omartian looks back at the trials, joys, and power found in praying for her kids. In 30 easy-to-read chapters, Stormie shares from personal experience how you can pray effectively for your children.

THE MOM I WANT TO BE
Rising Above Your Past to Give Your Kids a Great Future

T. Suzanne Eller

ISBN: 978-0-7369-1755-1

Your experience as a mother is influenced by the mothering you received. If inconsistency or neglect was a part of that upbringing, you need a healthier vision of how wonderful motherhood can be.

Suzie Eller compassionately shows how you can turn from a painful past and become the mom you want to be.

10-MINUTE TIME OUTS FOR YOU AND YOUR KIDS
Scriptures, Stories, and Prayers You Can Share Together

Grace Fox

ISBN: 978-0-7369-1860-2

These brief devotions pack excitement and encouragement to help you explore God's Word in a way that's
perfectly suited to all ages:

- *Read the Clue*—share a key verse for the day
- *Discover the Treasure*—hear a brief story and the truth
  it portrays
- *Share the Wealth*—offer a Scripture-based prayer and work
  on a question or activity
- *Hide a Jewel*—memorize a verse that reinforces the day's
  theme

In ten minutes a day, your family can become rich with the truth
about who God is and how He wants His children to live.

MAMA SAID THERE'D BE DAYS LIKE THIS
Refreshing Rest Stops for Moms on the Run

Jenn Ducette

ISBN: 978-0-7369-1939-5

Jenn Doucette, author of *The Velveteen Mommy*—and a
mother, of course—uses the joys, frustrations, and com-
edies of motherhood to reveal vital keys to keeping your
sanity: setting boundaries and achieving freedom; getting a grip on
emotions; finding time—even 5 minutes—to be alone; and more. This
fresh look at the delights and quandaries you face every day as a mom
will help you experience God's grace and love in a new way.

Read sample chapters of these and other good books
at www.harvesthousepublishers.com